DISCARD

NONNA'S HOUSE

NONNA'S HOUSE

COOKING AND REMINISCING WITH
THE ITALIAN GRANDMOTHERS OF
ENOTECA MARIA

JODY SCARAVELLA

WITH ELISA PETRINI

FEATURING THE NONNAS'
CLASSIC RECIPES

ATRIA BOOKS
NEW YORK LONDON TORONTO SYDNEY NEW DELHI

ATRIA BOOKS

A Division of Simon & Schuster, Inc.
1230 Avenue of the Americas
New York, NY 10020

First Atria Books hardcover edition April 2015

ATRIA BOOKS and colophon are trademarks of Simon & Schuster, Inc.

For information about special discounts for bulk purchases, please contact Simon & Schuster Special Sales at 1-866-506-1949 or business@simonandschuster.com.

The Simon & Schuster Speakers Bureau can bring authors to your live event. For more information or to book an event, contact the Simon & Schuster Speakers Bureau at 1-866-248-3049 or visit our website at www.simonspeakers.com.

Designed by Suet Yee Chong

Manufactured in China

10 9 8 7 6 5 4 3 2 1

Library of Congress Cataloging-in-Publication Data

Nonna's house : cooking and reminiscing with Italian grandmothers at Enoteca Maria / [compiled by] Jody Scaravella with Elisa Petrini.
    pages cm
Summary: "Recipes and stories from the Italian grandmothers who cook at Enoteca Maria"—Provided by publisher.
  Includes bibliographical references and index.
  1. Cooking, Italian. 2. Enoteca Maria. I. Scaravella, Jody. II. Petrini, Elisa.
T X723.N546 2015
641.5945—dc23
                                2014044839

ISBN 978-1-4767-7411-4
ISBN 978-1-4767-7413-8 (ebook)

This book is dedicated, with love and gratitude, to:

The memory of my Nonna Domenica,
for upholding centuries of tradition and sharing them with me.

The memory of my parents, Maria and John,
for giving me a solid foundation and keeping me
from getting too wild.

The memory of my sister, Marianna,
a wonderful cook, who left us much too soon.

My brother, John, a lover of food.

My two boys, Jesse and Jon,
who endured many bad meals as I was honing my kitchen skills.

Francesca Leone, who taught me so much about food and without
whom I never would have conceived the dream of the Enoteca.

CONTENTS

V CEREALI, RISO e GNOCCHI ROSA TURANO   75

VI PASTA ROSARIA VIGORITO   99

‹‹– I –››

BENVENUTI all' ENOTECA MARIA

Jody Scaravella

What connection runs deeper than food and family? I can't think of one more strongly reinforced from birth through every day of your life as you grow up. When you taste something you remember, it awakens your sense of identity, reminding you of where you came from. It ignites memories of being cared for or even spoiled—memories of your family's love.

My nonna, sister, and mother, 1949

These ideas were rattling around somewhere in my mind when I founded Enoteca Maria, a restaurant where the chefs are not professionals but *nonnas*, or Italian grandmothers. Each nonna embodies food wisdom and traditions that have been handed down for generations. They make me thankful for my own rich heritage, and I've seen the same gratitude and sense of connection, sometimes tearful, in people of every background who've enjoyed a meal with us.

But when I got the idea for the restaurant, I wasn't really conscious of my motivations. It all happened serendipitously. I lived in Brooklyn for fifty years, on the block where I grew up, with my parents and my sister right across the street. My brother moved away; and I lost my grandfather and father, my grandmother and mother, and my sister in fairly quick succession. I was feeling bereft, like the last man standing, and I'd inherited a little bit of money.

Waterfront land seemed like a great investment. That idea brought me to Staten Island, where the coastline is fairly open. The real estate broker asked, "Do you want to see an amazing house, just for fun? It has the best view in the borough."

"Sure," I said. But on the way, I told her, "Stop the car!"

We'd passed a little Dutch colonial house with a FOR SALE sign. It turned out to be a hundred years old. It, too, had a phenomenal view, but what grabbed me was the fact that the dining room had an old-fashioned picture rail—molding on the walls, about a foot down from the ceiling, ringing the room. My mother had collected Norman Rockwell plates, which were left to me in a cache of her belongings. The picture rail in that dining room struck me as just the place to display them. If you believe in signs, that had to be one. That day, I bought the house.

My new house was walking distance from the Staten Island Ferry dock and the little village of shops clustered there. One day I spotted a storefront for rent next door to a majestic, beautifully restored theater. On weekends, the theater drew hundreds of concertgoers from all over, but especially from Manhattan. What could be more romantic on a Saturday night than riding the ferry under the stars to see a show?

That was a huge plus, but even the space itself seduced me. It just felt like a cozy little restaurant. An Italian restaurant. I realize now that I was unconsciously trying to fill gaps: to re-create the warmth of my close-knit Italian neighborhood in Brooklyn, which was by then a vanishing world; to reconnect with the embrace of the family I had lost. The restaurant, Enoteca Maria, named for my mother, has succeeded at least partly because, in our disconnected lives, that sense of longing for community and those same blank spaces exist in a lot of people.

What did I know about running a restaurant? Nothing. By day I work as a materials forecaster for the Metropolitan Transit Authority, stockpiling subway parts. But I did grow up in Italian Brooklyn, with my Sicilian maternal grandmother, Domenica, living four blocks away. She and my mother were both tremendous cooks and lovers of food.

When I was a kid, my Nonna Domenica was a sweet old lady who spoiled me and my sister and brother. I'd go over to her house, and she'd ask, "Are you hungry?" Yeah, sure, if she was cooking. She'd have a little aluminum pot on the stove, which she'd fill with water. Then she'd take a whole chicken and some vegetables out of the refrigerator, start chopping, turn on the flame, and in what seemed like minutes, ladle out a bowl of the best chicken soup you ever tasted.

My grandmother may have coddled us kids, but she had that Old World flintiness. Now and then I glimpsed it. Every single day, she shopped at the Italian food markets on Eighty-Sixth Street, which are Asian markets now. Sometimes I'd go with her. I loved the tumult and color of the markets, with all the vendors shouting, vying for customers. My grandmother would push her shopping cart around to different stands, where she felt free to sample the wares. If she bit into a promising plum and it didn't pass muster, she'd throw it down and move on. No one dared to protest or challenge her.

My grandmother's backbone also showed in the way she helped support the family. My grandfather was a barber, making a decent living, which my grandmother supplemented by working in a sewing mill—a sweatshop—and doing finishing work at home on her old treadle sewing machine. Thanks to her earnings, my grandparents bought their own home. Nonna Domenica was close to a hundred years old when she died about fifteen years ago.

While Nonna Domenica and my mother taught me to appreciate good food, I got a real culinary education from my longtime girlfriend, Francesca Leone. Growing up in Calabria, to pull her weight in the family, she had to master all the traditional arts—cooking and baking, wine-making, preserving vegetables and fruits, even olives, and curing meats like *capocollo* and *soppressata*. She shared these time-honored rituals with me.

In our house in Brooklyn, I dug out a room under the back porch to use as a cold cellar and smokehouse. To make the hard Italian sausage soppressata, Francesca and I would wake up at five in the morning to pick up fifty pounds of meat—a combination of pork butt, which is the shoulder, and ham, which is the haunch. You need both to get the right proportion of lean meat and fat. We'd put half the meat through the grinder on a very coarse setting and chop the other half by hand into little cubes for the right texture. Next, the ground and cubed meat went into a giant tub, to which we'd add a pound of salt, a few cups of paprika for color, and because Francesca is a spice-craving Calabrese, a few cups of hot red pepper.

Then the real work began: mixing the meat and seasonings with our hands—just turning and churning it in the tub, without stopping—for a solid hour. After that, the meat had to rest for an hour, and so did the exhausted chef.

Meanwhile, we'd turned the pig's intestine inside out, washed it extremely well, and soaked it in lemon water. This would be the casing for the soppressata. We'd stuff the intestine with the meat mixture, tie it with twine, and prick the sausage all over with a pin. Then we'd coil it in a basket, under dish towels, topped with a heavy weight—that's why it's called soppressata; it's pressed—leaving it in the cold room overnight. The weight would slowly squeeze out all the air.

Nonna Domenica, me, and my mother, 1962

In the morning we'd hang the flattened sausages on a makeshift rack I'd constructed by pounding nails though boards that were suspended from the ceiling of the room. For the next week, once or twice a day, I'd build a hardwood fire in the middle of the floor, then seal the room to let the meat cold-smoke and develop a hearty flavor. After smoking the meat, it had to hang on the rack to cure for thirty to forty days.

Finally, it was ready. The last step in preservation was to store the soppressata completely insulated from the air. We did this the traditional way, by submerging it in casks of cooking oil, until we got inspired to invest in the modern-day equivalent, a vacuum sealer.

The taste was like nothing you could ever buy in the store: salty, smoky, spicy, with an earthy sweetness. Yes, making that soppressata was a lot of work but that flavor is indelibly imprinted in my mind. One of Francesca's great gifts to me was that connection to the age-old customs of my forefathers—or should I say foremothers?

It's the foremothers, after all, who uphold the traditions we take for granted until they disappear. So I put an ad in *America Oggi*, the Italian-language paper, to find grandmothers. It read, in rough translation: *Do you want to get out of the house? To show what you know? To share the classic dishes you feed your family?*

The volume of responses amazed me. I invited the best prospects to my house in Staten Island for interviews. Those were like carnival days, like a Fellini movie: all these grandmothers showing up, with husbands and children, even little kids, carrying plates of food. The families helped out with the sales pitch: "My wife's *pasta e fagioli* is the best . . ." "You've got to have some polenta and rabbit . . ." "Try some of this . . ."

I was looking for authenticity, to preserve vanishing traditions. The shape of that heritage varies by region. Italian customs and cuisine are strictly local, changing even from village to village. So, while there are lots of southern Italians in New York, making fantastic food, I tried to cast a wide net. We've had nonnas from Sicily and Campania in the south; Abruzzo in the center; and, representing the north, Veneto, Emilia-Romagna, and Lombardy, among other places. I don't second-guess their choices.

Instead, when the nonnas come to cook at the Enoteca, I tell them, "Look in the refrigerator and see what you feel like making." Half the time, I never know what we're serving on a given night, until I get there after my day job. The nonnas jokingly call me the boss, but we all know that I'm the boss in name only. The nonnas are the stars.

Besides soppressata, Jody and I made capocollo, which is much less work, though the meat is hard to find. In Italy, of course, we butchered our hogs, and we'd cure the nape of the neck—*capo* means "head" and *collo* means "neck"—so it wouldn't go to waste. In America, though, people use more common cuts of pork, like the loin or shoulder. It might taste good, but it's not what Italians mean by capocollo.

The traditional way is to take the back of the pig's neck and cure it with salt, in a cold place, for three or four days. Then you rub the inner surface with spices like paprika and cayenne pepper, and roll it up the long way. Cover the roll with cheesecloth—we'd use skin from the pig's ribs in Italy—tie it with twine, give it a light smoke, then hang it in the cold room for three or four months. That's all it takes. Real capocollo is a delicacy.

You see it in the way customers respond to them. I encourage the nonnas to come out of the kitchen and meet the guests, who'll jump up to hug and kiss them. Sometimes, at the end of the night, they give the nonna/chef a round of applause. It's magical. It's that absolutely primal connection between food and family. Whatever your background, the concept of having Nonna—a matriarchal figure, who holds the family together—in the kitchen, cooking for you, is just so powerful.

The nonnas are the reason why a little thirty-five-seat restaurant could gain a toehold in a city full of world-class Italian chefs. We have Lidia Bastianich, Mario Batali, Andrew Carmellini, Tom Colicchio—and that's just the beginning of the alphabet. They've all achieved greatness by reviving the old traditions—and, they'd be the first to admit, standing on the shoulders of the nonnas who cooked for them. At Enoteca Maria, we're bringing the nonnas into the spotlight and out from under their feet.

+ II +

CONSERVE

JODY SCARAVELLA *Traveling with Francesca, visiting small towns like hers in Calabria, has given me insight into Italy beyond what most tourists perceive. It's helped me understand the world of my immigrant grandparents and realize how brave they were to pioneer life in a new country.*

Francesca Leone

When I talk about my childhood, my kids can hardly believe it. I grew up in Calabria, the toe of the boot of Italy, in a town of maybe three hundred people. I was the third of five children, four girls and a baby brother. Our nonna lived five minutes away. She was a tough, tiny

Making soppressata in Brooklyn, 1995

woman, who always wore a hairnet. Back then, they had to be tough because life was hard.

Think about how she used to do laundry. She made her own soap from leftover lard. She'd lug the clothes down to a nearby stream to wash them, beating them against the rocks to get them clean. She didn't have bleach for white things, so she'd put them in a basket, covered with a rag and topped with a mixture of water and ashes from the fireplace. After letting them sit, she'd hang them in the sun to complete the whitening process.

Even after she got a gas stove, my nonna liked cooking the way she was taught, in the fireplace. There was often an iron pot of white beans or chickpeas sitting in the embers, simmering all day. When the beans were soft, she'd serve them with pasta in a classic Calabrian version of *pasta e fagioli* or alone with a simple sauce of onions, basil, olive oil, and rosemary, dusted with cheese. If she had some pancetta or a prosciutto skin, she'd use that to flavor the sauce. In the springtime, she'd cook fresh fava beans with a piece of pigskin that had been preserved in lard all winter. Those beans were so delicious—real comfort food.

In the summer, when there was no school, I loved to help her bake bread. She'd create her own starter with yeast, flour, warm water, and salt, setting it aside for days to develop. She'd mix some starter with flour and water and knead the dough for what seemed like an hour before putting it someplace warm—like under a blanket—to rise overnight. In the morning she'd form the dough into round loaves, then let it rise again while she did chores and stoked her brick oven with wood. To test the heat, she'd slip in a pancake-size circle of dough on her long wooden paddle. If it puffed up and colored like pita bread, the oven was ready.

When my nonna got older, my mother took over the baking, and now my little brother upholds the tradition of making bread. My brother also makes lard the way we did growing up, when slaughtering a pig was an occasion for celebration. To make lard, we'd collect the scraps from butchering—the fat, skin, organs, and bones—and put it all in a big cauldron. With a cup of water and a tablespoon of salt, we'd stew the mixture over low heat so the fat would dissolve without frying. We'd wind up with a pot of clear lard, to be jarred and stored in the cold cellar. We'd save the bones and scrape out the marrow to spread on bread.

But the best part was eating the lard-poached scraps, called *frittole*. We'd pepper them and serve them on a big platter with orange slices. My grandfather used to sauté frittole with eggs, which today people would call a heart attack in a pan. But is cooking with lard that much worse than eating bacon? Besides, we didn't eat meat all the time, the way Americans do, so it wasn't likely that a little lard would kill you.

The other big difference about our meat was that the animals ate real food. We fed the pigs chestnuts, bran, and figs and the chickens watermelon rind and dried bread, along with our leftovers. That gave the meat real flavor. What we didn't raise ourselves, my father got by hunting and fishing. When he caught anchovies, he'd gut them on the spot and rinse them in seawater. At home, we'd preserve them in salt, in earthenware crocks. Once he came home with a bag of eels, all about eighteen inches long. He told me to put them in the sink, so I did, and, being a kid, forgot them. The next thing you know, I felt something under my feet. Oh, no—there were eels all over the house! What a nightmare.

Another scary thing: My father would go hunting and bring home quail on a string. If you touched them, you'd find that some were still alive. That grossed me out. These stories may sound cruel to modern ears. But this is the way of the world, the truth behind the plastic packages in the supermarket.

My mother's cousin in traditional dress for Easter, 1946

Doing the dirty work yourself—taking responsibility for it—gives you a different kind of gratitude and reverence for your food.

Until I got married, I'd never left my family. I met my husband when he came to our village on his yearly visit, having moved to the States when he was four years old. By the time we met, everyone our age was trying to escape their villages, heading to cities like Milan or, like me with my husband, to New York.

America was a shock—even Bensonhurst, which was all Italian, where we lived with my in-laws in their five-bedroom house. Finally we got our own apartment, which seemed so small—just a living room, bedroom, and dining room—compared with how we lived in Italy. But I adjusted. My husband and I had two kids, but sadly, the marriage didn't last.

After we divorced I met Jody. The first time I opened the fridge at his family's house, I was shocked to see overcooked pasta. And they were Italian. "How can you eat that?" I asked. "It's not al dente."

Luckily, he laughed, and that's probably what got us cooking together. Sharing the knowledge I grew up with was fun, and it bonded us. Eventually Jody and I broke up, and I remarried a wonderful man, an angel, George Lecznar. He passed away not long ago of pancreatic cancer.

With George, I settled in Pennsylvania, not far from New York City, where I have a huge garden with every vegetable you can imagine. At the end of the season, I preserve the harvest for the winter, channeling the spirit of my nonna. I remember watching her cut plum tomatoes in half, then setting them out on a wicker tray to dry for a week in the sun. She did the same with eggplant and zucchini, cut in very thin slices. For tomato paste, she'd cook the tomatoes with salt, then strain them onto a platter, to be left outdoors in the sun for three or four days to thicken. Then she'd jar the paste, top it with olive oil and a layer of grape leaves, and seal the jars with waxed paper tied with string.

Of course, nowadays I have it so much easier than my nonna. For my eggplant and zucchini, I use a dessicator; and I blanch and freeze my beans. So, though I'm grateful to know the traditional ways, it's really no wonder that they're being lost. Even my little Italian hometown is changing, with the old cobblestone streets paved over to ease the way for cars.

CUT BLACK OLIVES OLIVE FRINGHIATE

4½ pounds

FRANCESCA LEONE ✳ This is a classic Calabrese way to prepare olives. Though the ingredients I use are similar, I handle black and green olives differently. Look for raw black olives at Italian markets or online.

4½ pounds large, firm, raw **black olives**
9 cups **kosher salt**, or as needed
6 fresh **peperoncini**
2 tablespoons **fennel seeds**

1 tablespoon **red pepper flakes**
3 **garlic** cloves
Extra-virgin **olive oil**

1. Wash the olives under cold running water in a large colander. With a small sharp knife, make four cuts on each olive from tip to tip.

2. Place the olives in a large bowl and cover with water. Rinse and drain two or three more times, then cover with warm water and stir in ½ cup of the salt. Drain and rinse three times a day, adding ½ cup salt each time to the fresh water, until the olives are no longer bitter, 5 to 6 days. Discard any olives that turn mushy during the process.

3. Position the rack in the center of the oven and preheat the oven to 200°F.

4. Drain the olives and spread them out on a large, rimmed baking sheet. Stir in 1 tablespoon salt, the peperoncini, and fennel seeds. Bake until warm and soft, about 30 minutes.

5. Cool the olives to room temperature on the baking sheet, about 1 hour. Transfer them with the peperoncini, fennel seeds, red pepper flakes, and garlic cloves to sterilized glass jars. Cover fully with oil, seal, and set aside for an hour or two to blend the flavors. Enjoy warm or store in a cool, dark place for about 2 months.

CRACKED GREEN OLIVES OLIVE SCHIACCIATE

4½ pounds

FRANCESCA LEONE ✳ The process for curing green olives is easier than the one for the black olives. I like to crack these in the traditional way, with a wooden mallet, but you could do it on a large cutting board with the bottom of a heavy pot. You can find raw green olives at Italian markets or online.

4½ pounds large, firm, raw **green olives**
9 cups **kosher salt**, or as needed
1 tablespoon **fennel seeds**
4 **garlic** cloves, minced, plus peeled
   whole cloves as needed

2 fresh **peperoncini**, chopped, plus
   whole peperoncini as needed
Distilled white **vinegar**
Extra-virgin **olive oil**

1. Spread the olives on a cutting board and crack open each one with a wooden mallet. Place them in a large bowl and submerge in warm water. Stir in ½ cup of the salt. Set aside overnight at room temperature.

2. Drain and rinse the olives, return them to the bowl, and cover with fresh water and another ½ cup salt. Repeat this process three times a day, adding fresh water and ½ cup salt each time, until the olives are sweet, not bitter, 5 to 6 days.

3. Drain the olives, rinse well, and return them to the bowl. Add the fennel seeds, minced garlic, and chopped peperoncini. Stir well and set aside to blend the flavors for 1 hour. They can be eaten now or kept, covered, in the refrigerator for 2 weeks.

4. To preserve the olives longer, sprinkle the olive mixture liberally with distilled white vinegar and spoon it into a fresh, clean cheesecloth bag. Set a heavy saucepan or roasting pan on top of the bag, set the bag and its weight in an even larger roasting pan or bucket, and set aside overnight to press all liquid out of the olives. When the olives are flattened and dry, pack them tightly into sterilized glass jars. Cover with oil to submerge fully, adding whole garlic cloves and peperoncini to each jar. Seal with sterilized lids and rings and store in a cool, dry place for up to 2 months.

STUFFED HOT GREEN PEPPERS

PEPERONCINI VERDI LUNGHI

 about 12 servings

FRANCESCA LEONE ※ These stuffed peppers are worth waiting a week and a half for. They're delicious alone or on a slice of crusty Italian bread.

24 small thin **hot green peppers** (about 2½ pounds), such as fresh hot peperoncini or friggitelli
¾ cup **fennel seeds**

¾ cup minced **garlic** (about 4 heads)
Extra-virgin **olive oil**
48 **anchovy fillets** packed in oil

1. Split the peppers on one side from the stem end to the bottom; carefully open them, keeping them intact. Remove the veins and seeds. Wash and dry the peppers.

2. Place the fennel seeds and garlic in a food processor; pulse several times, drizzling in just enough oil to make a paste. Stuff each pepper with 1 tablespoon of the fennel mixture as well as 2 anchovy fillets; fold closed.

3. Layer and tightly pack the stuffed peppers into a large glass or ceramic container. Lay a sheet of waxed paper over the peppers; set a heavy weight (such as a large can or two of tomatoes) on top. Refrigerate for 3 days, tilting the container and pressing on the weight to drain any liquid off the bottom once a day.

4. Remove the waxed paper and weight. Pour oil into the container to cover the peppers completely, with no air pockets. (To eliminate air pockets, stick the handle of a wooden spoon into the jar and work the air pocket to the surface.) Cover tightly and refrigerate for 1 week before serving. The peppers may be stored (fully covered in the oil) in the refrigerator for up to 2 weeks. If the oil solidifies, leave the jar out at room temperature for half an hour.

SUN-DRIED TOMATOES FILLED WITH ANCHOVIES AND CAPERS POMODORI SECCHI E RIPIENI SOTT'OLIO

 6 to 8 servings

FRANCESCA LEONE ✳ My nonna dried tomatoes in a flat basket in the sun. Their flavor was amazing! But with capers, anchovies, basil, and fennel, the sun-dried tomatoes at your store can be almost as irresistible.

8 ounces **sun-dried tomatoes** (dry packed, not in oil)

12 canned **anchovy fillets** packed in oil, halved

12 to 16 fresh **basil** leaves, halved, or as needed

2 tablespoons **nonpareil capers** in brine, drained

2 tablespoons **fennel seeds**

2 **garlic** cloves, thickly sliced

Extra-virgin **olive oil**

1. Place the sun-dried tomatoes in a very large bowl, cover with warm water, and set aside for 1 hour. Drain the tomatoes in a colander, rinse quickly, drain very well, and pat very dry with paper towels.

2. If using butterflied sun-dried tomatoes, fill one side of each tomato half with an anchovy fillet, half a basil leaf, a few capers, and a few fennel seeds; fold over the other side of the tomato to cover. If using the halved kind, top one tomato half with these ingredients, then lay a second tomato half on top, pressing gently to sandwich them together.

3. Layer the filled tomatoes in sterilized 1-quart canning jars, adding garlic cloves and more basil as you fill it. Press out any air before adding enough oil to cover the tomatoes completely. Use the handle of a wooden spoon to release any air pockets.

4. Seal the jars with sterilized lids and rings and store in a cool, dry place for 3 to 4 days to cure before serving. The tomatoes will keep, covered, in the refrigerator for up to 3 weeks. If the oil solidifies, leave the jar out at room temperature for half an hour.

EGGPLANT in OIL and VINEGAR

MELANZANE SOTT'OLIO E ACETO

FRANCESCA LEONE ✳ Eggplant is a delicious and unexpected accent on an antipasto platter. Sometimes my nonna would preserve a lot of vegetables together, like eggplant, olives, hot peppers, and mushrooms. Then, while she was cooking, she'd dip into the jar and add a scoop to whatever was in the pan to give it a boost of flavor. She taught me that if you want to use just some of the preserved food in a jar, remove it with a clean utensil, never your fingers. Otherwise, the rest of the batch will spoil.

2 medium Italian **eggplants** (about 1½ pounds), peeled and cut lengthwise into ¼-inch-thick slices
¼ cup **kosher salt**, or as needed
White wine vinegar
Extra-virgin **olive oil**

2 small fresh **hot peppers**, such as serrano chiles or hot red cherry peppers, seeded and chopped
3 **garlic** cloves, thinly sliced
1 tablespoon **fennel seeds**

1. Stack the eggplant in a bowl, sprinkling each layer liberally with salt. Set a plate on top and place a heavy weight such as large cans of tomatoes on the plate (you want the weight distributed evenly). Set aside overnight at room temperature to remove as much water as possible from the eggplant.

2. The next day, drain, rinse, gently squeeze, and pat dry the eggplant to remove any excess moisture. Wash the bowl, return the eggplant to the bowl, and sprinkle abundantly with vinegar. Set aside at room temperature for 2 hours, turning the slices occasionally. Working in batches, gently squeeze out as much of the vinegar as you can.

3. Layer the eggplant in a sterilized 2-quart glass container, sprinkling each layer with oil, hot peppers, garlic, and fennel seeds. Press down to remove all the excess air. Cover fully with oil, seal the jar with a sterilized lid and ring, and store in a dark, cool place for 3 to 4 days before serving. The eggplant will keep, covered, in the refrigerator for up to 2 weeks. If the oil solidifies, leave the jar out at room temperature for half an hour.

←← III →→

MINESTRE e ANTIPASTI

JODY SCARAVELLA *Any day of the week, I could make a meal of soup or antipasti. I love the variety—little bites of this and that—and the different textures and colors. My Nonna Domenica would set out an antipasto spread guaranteed to spoil your dinner: olives, cured meats and cheeses, wonderful artisanal bread, and fried cardoons, which were the best. But somehow we always managed to find room for the tempting courses that followed.*

Carmelina Pica

My mother used to say, "I always had a child in my arms, a child in my belly, and another one holding my hand." I come from a family of fourteen kids, nine of whom are alive today, five girls and four boys. I'm the fourth in line.

At sixteen in Marcianise, 1952

We were proud of our big family. When visitors dropped by, they'd usually find us gathered at the table, talking, kidding around, or even arguing, and they'd say, "Oh, what a beautiful sight." Sometimes they'd add, "You must have God's blessing to be able to feed all those mouths." We weren't rich—my father did financial work, for a bank and for the post office—but we never felt deprived of anything.

We lived in Marcianise, in the Campania region of southern Italy, about halfway between Caserta, the capital of our province, and Naples, the big city. When I was growing up, it was a town of just a few thousand people; today, there are more than ten times that many.

Naturally, with so many children, my mother was always at the stove. By the time she made us breakfast and did the dishes, it was time to cook our lunch. Luckily, my mother never had to leave the house. A cart would come by each morning with fruits and vegetables for sale. Since we lived on the second floor, my mom would go out on the terrace, shout down her order, then lower a basket for the vendor to fill with food.

Our terrace was big enough for a grape arbor, giving it a ceiling of vines, and a brick oven, where we baked bread. We kept our bread starter in the closet, ripening, and each week we'd break off a chunk to mix with flour and water for dough. That terrace became a dramatic setting in my life. That's where Pasquale, the man I would marry, first saw me.

I knew him, vaguely. Our families were connected through my aunt, who lived across the street. But most of Pasquale's family, including his parents, had immigrated to America, and since he worked on a ship, Pasquale traveled back and forth.

When he was ready to get married, his relatives found him a fiancée from a wealthy family. Though they'd never met, Pasquale came home to Italy fully prepared, with a wedding gown, the papers, and everything. Arranged marriages were very common back then, and many worked out well. But Pasquale and the girl didn't hit it off. So he broke off the engagement, went to stay with my aunt, and noticed me shaking my dust rag off the terrace.

Something about that struck him, because he told my aunt, "That's what I want. That's exactly the kind of girl I'm going to marry."

Pasquale persuaded my aunt to bring him to our house, where she told my parents, "You know, he's crazy about Carmelina."

My father said, "Maybe we can arrange something."

They sent me to the kitchen to make coffee. I came back with the serving tray and learned that I had a fiancé.

I cried and cried. Not so much about getting engaged—I was twenty-three, old enough to want to start a family—as about leaving home and moving to America. My father understood, but he encouraged me. "You've never even had a boyfriend," he said, "so you don't know what it's like. But you're going to fall in love with Pasquale."

He was right. We got engaged in July, spent a few months getting to know each other, and on November 13, we were married. A few years ago, Pasquale and I celebrated our fiftieth wedding anniversary.

I sailed to America alone—nine days on the boat—and arrived on a Friday. Pasquale brought me to his mother's house in Jamaica, Queens. But I had no time for culture shock or new-bride panic because, on Monday—three days later—my new husband was nabbed by the FBI.

At the time, all young men living in America had to serve in the military. Pasquale registered for the draft, as required, which meant that he could be conscripted at any time until he turned twenty-six. Because of his poor English, they initially passed him over and then, apparently, sent a call-up notice when Pasquale was away at sea. Now the government was at the door, calling him a deserter. They hauled him off and shipped him out to an American base in Korea.

There I was, a newlywed, living in a strange country, with a mother-in-law I'd barely met. Can you imagine? But luckily, Pasqualina, my mother-in-law, welcomed me like a daughter. She taught me to make her specialties—her tagliatelle, her pappardelle, her gnocchi, her beans with prosciutto and pigskin. My mother had made similar dishes but, with so many kids running around, she was usually too busy to show

With Pasquale on our wedding day

us how. During the two and a half years we lived together, I grew to love Pasqualina dearly, and when she grew older, I took care of her until the day she died.

But with Pasquale gone, I cried all the time out of homesickness. My departure was equally wrenching for my family. Just before I sailed, my father handed me a letter, saying, "Read this when you get settled." It began, "You leave a huge hole in my heart . . ."— words that still move me to tears.

Less than five years later, my father fell ill, and I rushed back to Italy. His surprise and joy at seeing me revived him briefly. He swore that he'd get better and visit me in America, "even if I have to fly outside the plane, even if I have to grab its tail, I'm coming!" He also insisted that I cook for him: "I want to eat something American from you!" I made him beef stew, American-style, over rice, which he loved. A short time later, he passed away, at sixty-three.

What helped me find my footing in America, with Pasquale in Korea, was dressmaking. Many Italian kids of my generation (and past ones) got after-school lessons from local experts in what you might call life skills. Girls, typically, had sewing classes, and boys learned shoe repair. When I was in my late teens, I'd become a sewing teacher and on the side did custom tailoring—nothing expensive, since no one was rich. I even made my own wedding gown. It was a nice little business. In America, it struck me that I had a marketable skill so I went to work in a sewing factory.

I saved most of my earnings, along with my military spouse stipend. When Pasquale came home from Korea, we had a big enough nest egg to get our own apartment in Queens. We lived there for twenty-two years and raised a beautiful family: three children, Michael, Tony, and Patrice, who now have kids of their own, Jacques Anthony, Camilla, and Carmelina and Caterina, who are twins.

Most of us, it seems, have found our way into the food world. Patrice's husband, Jacques, who's French, had a restaurant called San Michel in Bay Ridge, Brooklyn, before partnering with Michael, my oldest, on a new place, Frère Jacques, in midtown Manhattan. Tony, my second son, brought Michael into a venture called Almonds Cafe in Port Charlotte, Florida. Then one of Pasquale's brothers, Bruno, along with my mother-in-law, moved to Staten Island, where he headed a franchise of the A&S Pork Store, a well-known Italian market. The store does catering and has a big line of takeout foods—hero sandwiches, stuffed pizzas and breads, Italian salads and desserts, as well as an array of hot and cold Italian appetizers that have become its hallmark.

Twenty-seven years ago, I started to help Bruno with the appetizer business. For catering, the food has to be predictable, but with appetizers, you can get creative. I discovered how much I liked improvising—just adding a little of this or that. For example, one day there were some beautiful red peppers in the store. I decided to cut them into strips and started mixing in ingredients like garlic and parsley, capers and pignoli, chopped Gaeta olives, and olive oil before roasting them and topping them with breadcrumbs. We called my creation Stuffed Pepper Strips, and it was an instant hit with customers. It's a dish that Bruno credits with making the store famous.

Another is the seafood salad I came up with. Everyone has a version, but mine is unusual, as it's especially beautifully

My whole family in Marcianise, 1960

colored. My salad is so popular that every year, many Staten Island families make it a staple of their Christmas Eve dinner. The store sells at least five hundred pounds of it then and still can't fill all the orders.

The work was hard, but I enjoyed it so much. It was rewarding. Pasquale used to say, "Put you in the kitchen, Carmelina, and you're in glory."

Now we're retired. Pasquale and I spend winters in Florida, and when we're up north, I cook at the Enoteca, just for the joy of it. It's the kind of improvisational cooking I love. I never come with a fixed idea but check the menu the day before, so I can come up with different dishes. It's creative.

The customers are so appreciative. Once a guest sketched a cartoon of me, in my smock, while I was cooking. I didn't even know until he came back another day to show me, saying, "Here, this is for you." That was so charming.

You know what's funny? Pasquale is my toughest customer. He'll say, "How come you make it that way? Why don't you add a little more of this?" He likes to criticize. Once we had a big fight, and he threw his food right into the garbage pail. "You just want to bring me down," I told him. "Everyone else I cook for puts me up on a pedestal."

But he's a good man, even if he's picky by nature. He's proud of my cooking and knows he can't deny that it has made a lot of people happy. You just think you can get away with things, like saying whatever you want, when you've been married as many years as we have.

MARRIED SOUP MINESTRA MARITATA

about 8 servings

ADELINA ORAZZO ✳ This soup was my father's specialty, made for holidays like Christmas. Almost every Neapolitan family makes some version of it. Although the translation of its name is "married soup," it has nothing to do with marriage. Instead, the name refers to the way separately cooked ingredients finally unite into a delicious meal.

1 teaspoon **salt**
8 ounces boneless **beef chuck**
1½ pounds bone-in, skin-on **chicken thighs**
1 large **pig's foot**, cleaned by the butcher
8 ounces **pork tenderloin**

3 cups chopped green **cabbage**
1½ cups chopped **escarole**
1½ cups chopped **dandelion greens**
½ teaspoon freshly ground **black pepper**
Extra-virgin **olive oil**, for garnish
Finely grated **Pecorino Romano**, for garnish

1. Fill a large soup pot or Dutch oven with 4 quarts water. Stir in the salt until dissolved, add the beef, and bring to a boil. Cover, reduce the heat, and simmer until the beef is tender, about 1 hour. Transfer the beef to a large bowl and refrigerate.

2. Add the chicken thighs to the pot. Raise the heat and bring the liquid back to a boil. Cover, reduce the heat, and simmer until the chicken is tender, about 45 minutes. Transfer the chicken to the bowl with the beef. Pour the stock into a bowl, cover, and refrigerate.

3. Place the pig's foot in the same pot, fill the pot with water, and bring to a boil. Cover, reduce the heat, and simmer until the pig's foot is tender, 2 to 3 hours. Transfer the pig's foot to the bowl with the beef and chicken. Discard the water in the pot.

4. Put the pork tenderloin in the same pot, fill the pot with water, and bring to a boil. Reduce the heat and simmer until cooked through, about 12 minutes. Transfer the tenderloin to the bowl with the other meats.

5. Remove the stock from the refrigerator and skim the fat; pour the stock into the pot. Stir in the cabbage, escarole, dandelion greens, and pepper. Bring to a simmer, stirring often. Cook until the greens are tender, about 15 minutes.

6. Meanwhile, chop the beef and pork tenderloin into ½-inch pieces. Skin and debone the chicken thighs and pig's foot; chop the meat into small pieces. Mix the meats together.

7. Bring the pot of soup to a full boil. Divide the meat mixture among eight serving bowls; ladle the very hot soup and greens on top. Drizzle with oil and sprinkle with Pecorino Romano to serve.

NORTHERN-STYLE MINESTRONE

MINESTRONE DEL NORD

 6 to 8 servings

CHRISTINA NARISI CARROZZA ✳ Minestrone is a free-form soup, the chance to use up whatever vegetables you have around. In northern Italy, we often use beets, a popular crop (but a real surprise to people used to minestrone from farther south). They give the soup a gorgeous color and a little sweetness.

1 large russet **potato**, peeled and diced (about 2 cups)

1 (15-ounce) can **cannellini beans**, drained and rinsed

2 large **carrots**, diced (about 1¾ cups)

2 medium red **beets**, peeled and diced (about 1 cup)

1 large **leek**, white and pale green parts only, diced (about ⅔ cup)

2 medium **celery** stalks, diced (about 1 cup)

3 **garlic** cloves, minced

1 large **zucchini**, diced (about 2 cups)

1 cup medium-grain **white rice**, such as arborio

5 tablespoons extra-virgin **olive oil**

¼ cup chopped fresh **basil**

¼ cup minced fresh **flat-leaf parsley**

1 teaspoon **salt**

½ teaspoon freshly ground **black pepper**

Finely grated **Parmigiano-Reggiano**, for garnish

1. Place the potato, beans, carrots, beets, leek, celery, and garlic in a Dutch oven or large soup pot. Add enough water so that the vegetables are just barely covered; bring to a boil. Cover, reduce the heat, and simmer for 1 hour.

2. Stir in the zucchini, rice, oil, basil, parsley, salt, and pepper. Continue simmering until the rice is tender, about 30 minutes. If the soup becomes too thick, add water as needed. Ladle into bowls to serve and garnish with Parmigiano-Reggiano.

CREPES IN BROTH CRESPELLE IN BRODO

6 servings

ROSARIA VIGORITO ✳ This dish, also known as *scrippelle imbusse*, is an Abruzzese specialty. The crepes can be made ahead: Let them cool to room temperature, fill them with cheese, and roll them up, then wrap them in plastic wrap and refrigerate for up to 12 hours before setting them in the bowls.

1 cup **all-purpose flour**, plus more as needed
5 ounces **Parmigiano-Reggiano**, finely grated (about 1¼ cups)
3 tablespoons minced fresh **flat-leaf parsley**, plus more for garnish
½ teaspoon **salt**
⅛ teaspoon grated **nutmeg**

4 large **eggs**, at room temperature
1 cup whole **milk**, plus more as needed
9 cups **chicken broth**, preferably homemade
Extra-virgin **olive oil**, for the pan
1½ ounces **Pecorino Romano**, finely grated (about ⅓ cup)

1. Whisk the flour, 2 tablespoons of the Parmigiano-Reggiano, the parsley, salt, and nutmeg in a large bowl. In a second large bowl, whisk the eggs and milk until smooth and uniform. Whisk the egg mixture into the flour mixture until smooth. The batter should have the consistency of heavy cream; add a little more flour if it's too thin or a little more milk if it's too pasty. Cover the bowl and refrigerate for 1 hour.

2. Pour the broth into a large saucepan and heat until bubbles form at the edges of the pan. Reduce the heat to very low, cover, and keep warm.

3. Heat a 6-inch nonstick skillet or crepe pan over medium-high heat for 2 minutes. Dab some oil on a paper towel, grasp it with kitchen tongs, and use it to lightly grease the pan. Pour 3 tablespoons of the batter into the pan and quickly tilt the pan to spread the batter evenly. Cook the crepe until golden on the bottom, 1 to 1½ minutes. Flip the crepe and cook until the other side is golden, less than 1 minute. Transfer the crepe to a plate and continue with the remaining batter, making about 18 crepes. When you notice the crepes sticking, oil the pan again.

4. Spread the crepes on a dry work surface and sprinkle them evenly with the remaining Parmigiano-Reggiano and all the Pecorino Romano. Roll the crepes into tight scrolls. To serve, arrange three crepes in each of six bowls. Ladle the hot broth on top and garnish with parsley.

ABRUZZO-STYLE FARRO SOUP WITH PANCETTA AND SAGE ZUPPA DI FARRO ALL'ABRUZZESE

 6 servings

ROSARIA VIGORITO ✳ I love farro as a side dish or added to a salad or a soup, as in this recipe. I've even eaten it as a dessert in some kind of mousse. Whole-grain farro can take a long time to cook, so I look for the kind that's called *semi-perlato* ("semi-pearled").

2 cups semi-perlato **farro**
6 tablespoons **olive oil**
1 medium **onion**, diced (about 1 cup)
2 ounces **pancetta**, diced
½ teaspoon **salt**
½ teaspoon freshly ground **black pepper**
½ tablespoon rubbed **sage**
1 **bay leaf**

1 cup canned diced **tomatoes**, chopped
8 cups **beef broth**, preferably homemade
Chopped fresh **flat-leaf parsley**, for garnish
Extra-virgin **olive oil**, for garnish
Finely grated **Parmigiano-Reggiano**, for garnish

1. Place the farro in a large bowl and cover with cold water. Soak for 2 hours, then drain.

2. Warm the oil in a large pot or Dutch oven set over medium heat. Add the onion, pancetta, salt, and pepper. Cook, stirring often, until the onion turns translucent, about 4 minutes. Do not brown. Stir in the sage and bay leaf and cook until fragrant, about 30 seconds.

3. Stir in the tomatoes and the farro. Pour in the broth, bring to a simmer, cover, stirring occasionally, until the farro is tender, 30 to 45 minutes. Serve in bowls, garnished with parsley, oil, and Parmigiano-Reggiano.

SNAILS PALERMO STYLE BABBALUCI PALERMITANI

ELVIRA PANTALEO ✳ My wedding party was a food extravaganza. A big pot of *babbaluci*, a Sicilian specialty, was one of the essentials that we served our guests.

2 pounds small live **snails**, cleaned
  (see note)
1 tablespoon **salt**
¼ cup extra-virgin **olive oil**

5 **garlic** cloves, minced
1 cup packed fresh **flat-leaf parsley**,
  chopped
½ teaspoon freshly ground **black pepper**

1. Place the snails in a deep pot and add water to cover by 4 inches. Set over high heat and bring to a boil. As soon as the snails begin to emerge from their shells, stir in the salt. Once the water is boiling, reduce the heat to low and cook, stirring occasionally, for 10 minutes. Drain and rinse well with cold water.

2. Warm the oil in a very large, deep skillet set over medium heat. Add the garlic and cook, stirring often, until lightly browned at the edges, about 20 seconds. Add the snails and continue cooking for 2 or 3 minutes to warm them through. Stir in the parsley and pepper just before serving right from the skillet or from a serving bowl.

◁ **NOTE** ▷ *You want small snails (not big French escargots). You can find them in Italian specialty markets or even Asian supermarkets. The snails can be muddy, so they need to be washed well. And they have a little hard bit (like a half-moon fingernail cutting) at the opening of the shell near the foot. Pick this off each one with a toothpick. Snails also have a tendency to wander away while you're getting ready to cook them. Rub the inside of a deep skillet with olive oil, then dust it with fresh breadcrumbs. Pour the snails inside, and they can't go anywhere.*

PASTA and BEANS with MUSSELS

PASTA E FAGIOLI CON COZZE

 4 to 6 servings

ADELINA ORAZZO ✳ This is one of my signature dishes at the Enoteca. Mussels give classic *pasta e fagioli* the flavor of Naples.

2 tablespoons **olive oil**

3 **garlic** cloves, crushed with a garlic press

½ teaspoon **red pepper flakes**, or to taste

1 pound **mussels**, cleaned and debearded

½ cup dry **white wine**

1 (28-ounce) can crushed **tomatoes**

1 cup **vegetable broth**

3 tablespoons minced fresh **basil**, plus more for garnish

1 tablespoon minced fresh **flat-leaf parsley**, plus more for garnish

½ teaspoon **salt**

½ teaspoon freshly ground **black pepper**

½ pound dried spiral **pasta**, cooked and drained

1 (14-ounce) can white **kidney beans**, drained and rinsed

1. Warm the oil in a large soup pot or Dutch oven set over medium heat. Stir in the garlic and red pepper flakes; cook until fragrant, about 30 seconds.

2. Add the mussels and wine. Cook, stirring occasionally, until the wine has evaporated, 3 to 4 minutes.

3. Add the tomatoes, broth, basil, parsley, salt, and pepper. Cover and cook until the mussels have opened, about 4 minutes.

4. Use a slotted spoon to transfer half the mussels to a large bowl; set aside. Reduce the heat and keep the ingredients in the pot at a bare simmer. Using tongs and a fork, take the remaining mussels in the pot out of their shells, letting the meat drop back into the broth and discarding the shells.

5. Raise the heat to medium; stir the cooked pasta and beans into the mussel sauce. Simmer for 1 minute to heat through. Divide the mixture among four to six bowls; top evenly with the reserved mussels in their shells. Garnish with basil and parsley.

STUFFED SARDINES SARDE A BECCAFICO

8 servings

TERESA SCALICI ※ Sardines are one of Sicily's most plentiful fish. We eat them on March 19 to honor St. Joseph, but we enjoy them the rest of the year, too. Here's my version of the traditional recipe.

6 tablespoons **olive oil**
Zest and juice of 1 medium **orange**
Zest and juice of 1 medium **lemon**
2 pounds fresh **sardines**, cleaned, heads and tails removed
1 medium **onion**, minced (about 1 cup)
3 cups fresh **breadcrumbs**

1 cup **red wine vinegar**
¾ cup **raisins**, chopped
¼ cup **sugar**
1 tablespoon chopped fresh **flat-leaf parsley**
½ teaspoon **salt**
½ teaspoon freshly ground **black pepper**

1. Whisk 2 tablespoons of the oil with the orange and lemon juices in a large bowl. Add the sardines, toss well, cover, and refrigerate for 30 minutes, stirring occasionally.

2. Heat a large skillet over low heat for a minute or two, then pour in 2 tablespoons more oil. Add the onion and cook, stirring often, until soft and golden, about 25 minutes. Remove from the heat; stir in the breadcrumbs, vinegar, raisins, sugar, parsley, salt, and pepper, as well as the orange and lemon zests. Let the mixture cool.

3. Meanwhile, position the rack in the center of the oven and preheat the oven to 350°F. Line a 9 x 13-inch baking dish with parchment paper.

4. Take about 2 tablespoons of the breadcrumb mixture, gently squeeze any excess vinegar back into the skillet, and stuff the mixture into a sardine. Close the fish and press down lightly. Lay the stuffed fish in the baking dish and continue stuffing the rest of the sardines, arranging them in a single layer in the dish. Pour any vinegar in the skillet over the sardines. Drizzle with the remaining 2 tablespoons oil.

5. Bake until hot and bubbling, 15 to 20 minutes. Serve hot or at room temperature.

WARM SEAFOOD SALAD

INSALATA CALDA DI FRUTTI DI MARE

 8 servings as a starter or 6 as a main course

NINA PICARIELLO ✳ The deep flavors of this traditional seafood salad come from cooking all the shellfish, one type at a time, in the same water. If you buy squid from a fish market, ask to have it cleaned. If you buy it frozen, it will be ready to use.

5 tablespoons **olive oil**
1 tablespoon minced **garlic**
1 pound **cherrystone clams**, scrubbed clean
1 pound **mussels**, scrubbed and debearded
1 pound small **squid**, cleaned and cut into ½-inch-thick rings

1 pound medium **shrimp** (about 30 per pound), peeled and deveined
2 tablespoons minced fresh **basil**
2 tablespoons fresh **lemon juice**
¼ teaspoon **salt**
¼ teaspoon freshly ground **black pepper**

1. Warm 3 tablespoons of the oil in a large saucepan set over medium heat, then add the garlic. Cook, stirring often, until lightly browned, about 2 minutes. Add the clams and 2 cups water. Cover and bring to a simmer. Cook undisturbed for 4 minutes.

2. Stir in the mussels. Cover and continue cooking until both mollusks have opened, about 5 minutes. Turn off the heat. Use tongs to remove the mollusks one at a time from the pot. Pick out the meat with a fork, drop it into a large serving bowl, discard the shell, and continue until you've removed the shells from all the clams and mussels. Discard any clam or mussel that has not opened.

3. Set the saucepan over medium-high heat and return the liquid to a boil. Add the squid, cover, reduce the heat, and simmer until cooked through and tender, about 9 minutes. Use a slotted spoon to transfer the squid to the bowl with the clams and mussels.

4. Add the shrimp. Cover and cook until pink and firm, about 4 minutes. Use a slotted spoon to transfer the shrimp to the bowl with the other shellfish. Discard the water in the pan.

5. Stir the remaining 2 tablespoons oil, the basil, lemon juice, salt, and pepper into the seafood salad. Serve warm.

SMOKED HERRING SALAD with ORANGES

INSALATA DI ARINGHE AFFUMICATE E ARANCE

4 servings

ELVIRA PANTALEO ✳ Fish with oranges is a classic Sicilian combination. The smokiness of the herring gives this salad a wonderful flavor.

2 whole **smoked herrings** (about 8 ounces each)
½ cup extra-virgin **olive oil**
6 small **oranges**, peeled, seeded, and chopped

4 medium **scallions**, thinly sliced
1 tablespoon fresh **lemon juice**
½ teaspoon freshly ground **black pepper**

1. Place the herring on a cutting board; slice off and discard the heads and tails. Peel off the skin, then scrape and peel the meat from the bones. Discard the bones.

2. With clean hands, shred the meat, letting it fall into a serving bowl. Add the oil, oranges, scallions, lemon juice, and pepper. Stir gently before serving.

MARINATED EELS CAPITONE ALLA SCAPECE

4 servings

NINA PICARIELLO ✳ This vinegar preparation for eels is the Italian version of *escabeche*. In fact, the sauce could be used with meat and vegetables, as well as fish. In southern Italy, eels are a favorite Christmas Eve appetizer.

½ cup **all-purpose flour**
1 teaspoon **salt**
1 teaspoon freshly ground **black pepper**
2 (1-pound) **eels**, gutted, skin removed, and flesh cut into 2-inch pieces (see note)

6 tablespoons **olive oil**, plus more as needed
2 tablespoons minced fresh **oregano**
2 teaspoons minced **garlic**
½ cup **red wine vinegar**

1. Mix the flour, salt, and pepper on a large plate. Dredge the eel pieces in the seasoned flour, shaking off any excess.

2. Warm 4 tablespoons of the oil in a medium skillet set over medium-high heat until rippling. Add several pieces of the eel and cook, turning occasionally, until golden on all sides, 4 to 5 minutes. Transfer to a 9 x 13-inch baking dish and continue cooking the remaining eel, adding more oil as needed but adding the eel only when the oil is hot.

3. Pour off all but 1 tablespoon of the oil from the skillet. Return the skillet to medium heat and add the oregano and garlic. Stir until fragrant, about 10 seconds. Pour in the vinegar and scrape up any browned bits from the bottom of the skillet as the vinegar begins to bubble. Pour the vinegar mixture over the eel. Drizzle with the remaining 2 tablespoons oil, cover, and refrigerate for 24 hours. Serve cold or at room temperature.

◁ **NOTE** ▷ *Buy eels that are alive and swimming. Have your fishmonger clean and gut them for you. You'll need to prepare the dish the minute you get home while the eels are still fresh.*

⤜ IV ⤛

VERDURE

JODY SCARAVELLA *For many Americans, meat is the center of a meal and vegetables are almost an afterthought. Of course, the opposite is true in the rest of the world. In Italian cooking, vegetables play a starring role.*

Nina Picariello

The morning after my wedding, I asked Gaetano, my new husband, "What do I make you for dinner?" I was puzzling out marriage, creating a home, and having a husband to keep happy.

Gaetano told me, "Make whatever you want. I'll never tell you

With my mother in Salerno, 1952

what to cook, and don't tell me ahead of time either. Let it be a surprise, and I'll look forward to whatever we're having."

The perfect answer.

But, over time, I discovered that there was something he really longed for: his mother's eggplant Parmesan. She'd passed away, taking her recipe with her, and his description was no help. Normally, of course, you simply salt and drain the eggplant; dip it in flour, egg, and breadcrumbs; fry it; layer it with sauce and mozzarella; and stick it in the oven. How do you improve on that? I kept trying, improvising little changes, but every time, he'd tell me, "No, this isn't right."

He'd say it playfully—it was a joke we shared—but the mystery was driving me crazy. Finally, I called his sister, begging, "Tell me your mother's secret. I can't take it anymore."

"Okay," she said. "But once I learned that recipe, I wished I'd never asked!"

Gaetano's mother would start out the usual way, then pack mozzarella between the fried eggplant slices—like grilled cheese sandwiches—redip them in the egg and breadcrumbs, refry them, and go from there, layering and baking. The process was messy, and it took forever.

But Gaetano was so excited when I served it. "You did it," he said. "How did you figure it out?"

I laughed, not about to admit that I'd called his sister, which would seem like cheating. "I'm not even telling you," I said. "But enjoy it, because this is the first and last time I'll ever make it."

In her later years, all my nonna would eat was what we called "cracked eggplant"— fried, and then stuffed with cherry tomatoes, parsley, basil, garlic, olives, and capers, before getting finished off in the oven. That was probably my favorite food, too, when I was eight or nine.

For most of my childhood, I lived in my nonna's home. It was on the outskirts of Salerno, which is in Campania, nestled between the Apennine Mountains and the Tyrrhenian Sea. But I was actually conceived in Rome, my father's posting in the armed forces. When the war broke out, he was deployed and my mother returned to Salerno to have me, her first child.

My maternal grandmother, a widow, ran a little general store that sold, among other things, eggs and live chickens. I grew up on those eggs, poking a hole in the shell to suck out the insides, which was supposed to make me big and strong. Our vegetables came from my nonna's garden, and barter was common in our close-knit community. Between that and what my mother earned working in a tobacco factory, we got by.

My paternal grandparents lived near us, and one day when I was five, out playing, I was summoned to their house. I was only told, "There's something going on." Rushing in, I saw all the adults I knew, along with a man I didn't recognize. A stranger who—I somehow grasped—was my father. Captured by the British, he'd spent four years in a prison camp. I ran to him and fell into his arms.

For a while, thanks to my father's war pension and his return to work as a barber, our lives got a bit more comfortable. When I was in my early teens, he and my mother gave me a little sister, Caterina. But the following year, my father, only forty, died from complications of an old war wound to his stomach. Again, my nonna welcomed us into her home—a new one near Lungomare Trieste, Salerno's seafront promenade. She'd come to believe that spirits infested her mountainside house—good or bad ones, she didn't know—and that in a more urban setting, haunting was less likely.

But I missed living on the mountain, where on Sundays, all the neighbors would come together for a meal, which lasted hours. On special occasions, they'd pitch in to roast a lamb, sharing every bit, from snout to hoof. My nonna always loved the head, a delicacy that today I make at the Enoteca. Families didn't see themselves as isolated units, as we do now.

I also missed the sense of family that a man brings to a house, even beyond mourning the loss of my father. A home needs a heart, a center. While my father was alive, even when we lived in my nonna's house, she was just the cocaptain of the ship. My father was the skipper, and keeping him happy gave us all a sense of purpose. A houseful of women—all working hard, eating together without a family's lively flow of guests—can seem grim and unfocused.

Then my mother fell in love and remarried, giving our lives a new compass.

Vittorio, my stepfather (I called him Papa), was a widower with two children, a boy and a girl. When I was about seventeen, he and my mother had a baby. Our expanded family moved from an ancient, dilapidated walk-up into a fresh postwar apartment in a four-story elevator building. Papa, an excellent cook, waiter, and manager, was well established in the restaurant world.

When I was twenty, he succeeded in opening his own place, the Golden Conch, a three-story restaurant with a staff of twenty. Soon it became one of Salerno's top dining spots, and my entire family plunged into the business. My job was washing linens, squeezing them through the mangle, then hanging them to dry overnight. In the morning I'd iron the napkins and press the tablecloths right in place, rather than folding them, to avoid wrinkles. My back ached from the labor, but I had an even greater ache in my heart—for Leonardo, the head chef.

He was from Abruzzo, one of Italy's famous food regions, and was so accomplished that he'd be hired to open restaurants, lending them his reputation and establishing their menus, before moving on and leaving the day-to-day operations to lesser and cheaper chefs. What struck me first about Leonardo were his hands—masculine but beautifully sensitive and precise as he prepared the *primi piatti*, or first plates—all the pastas, the ravioli, and the like. He'd say, "Nina, come help me. Let me show you how to do this . . . ," and I'd gasp for breath.

Powerful as our connection was, Leonardo and I never even kissed. Still, our bond was so strong that it grew obvious to others—including my stepfather, who slapped me. Then he went after Leonardo, outraged at his disrespect. "I want to marry your daughter," Leonardo said. "If you allow that, I'll work for you for free."

Instead of hearing him out, Papa fired Leonardo. I was shocked and heartsick. Papa thought that being such an acclaimed chef, Leonardo would be constantly on the move, launching restaurants. "I won't have you live like a gypsy!" Papa insisted.

I swallowed my grief, but Leonardo took the breakup hard. At one point I heard that he carried a knife and was threatening, "If I can't have Nina, no one else ever will." I was terrified. Finally, Leonardo disappeared.

Jump ahead many years: I happened to stop into a restaurant with one of my daughters, who was then nine. The cook, a bearded man, kept staring at us, which I ignored. But the next time I passed the place, he spotted me and asked. "Don't you know who I am?"

I must have looked confused. "I'm Leonardo," he said.

Leonardo! He'd aged, of course, and with the beard hiding his features, I barely recognized my old flame. "I never stopped loving you," he told me.

He reached into his pocket and drew out something shiny—not the knife I'd feared long ago, thank God. "This is the key to my home," he said. "I've kept it for you all these years."

As I tried to rush off, flustered, he pressed the key into my hand. When I next heard Leonardo's name, it was on a radio call-in show. He dedicated a Neapolitan love song to me. That outraged my husband. "What does he want?" Gaetano demanded. I didn't know the answer.

Eventually, Leonardo and his irrepressible passions faded from our lives. I've been asked, "Do you ever regret losing that big romance?" No. There's an expression

With my husband on vacation in Circeo, 1991

in Italian: *The big things you only do once, the small things you do all the time.* In other words, grand gestures count much less than little, everyday actions. I doubt that operatic passion like Leonardo's would hold up well in marriage, with its mundane challenges. But since our lives are the sum of our experiences, I feel lucky that deep and different kinds of love have colored mine.

Papa judged all my suitors strictly. He never wanted me exposed to a man who wasn't well educated, well groomed, well mannered and respectful, morally sound, and likely to be a good provider. At first even Gaetano didn't pass muster. Papa knew his father, so he formally introduced us and let Gaetano, then a budding engineer, begin the long courtship process. I really liked him but, after a year, Papa, unconvinced of his financial prospects, told me to send him away. As was expected back then, I obeyed.

A year later, we gave a big Carnevale bash at the restaurant. Gaetano pulled up in a beautiful car—clearly doing better than Papa had predicted—and asked me to dance. "I've thought of you all this time," he whispered. I'd been thinking of him, too. When the party ended, he kissed me good night and said, "I'm going to fight for you."

And he did, winning over Papa. We married on December 10, 1966—more than forty years ago. It was raining that day, giving proof to the saying *Sposa bagnata, sposa fortunata*: "A wet bride is a fortunate bride."

Within a month of our wedding, I was pregnant with my first daughter, Matilde, and within a year of her birth, I had another, Carla. As we settled into life in Salerno, Gaetano advanced in business and I found that I loved being a mother and a wife. A decade passed, and we were surprised but blessed by the birth of a son, Claudio.

By then my stepsister and her husband had settled in suburban New York, where they ran a business. When my daughter reached college age, she decided that, instead of school, she wanted to see what America had to offer. For me and Gaetano, raised according to strict traditions, it was almost unthinkable to let her go. But the world had changed. We had to be open-minded—and even more so when, a few years later, our other daughter also decided to emigrate.

I visited my daughters at least once a year. When they both married and were starting families, I had to wonder why I lived so far away. On one visit, I attended a New Year's Eve party. The first thing I saw was a huge ice sculpture, which was amazing, but what shocked me most was the buffet. Meats and cheeses, fruits and vegetables—all out of season—plus a vast array of shellfish. So I went a little crazy, eating everything in sight—then was stunned to hear that this was cocktail hour, with a full dinner still to come. Never in my life had I seen such abundance, not even at the most sumptuous wedding. I felt like a queen.

That's when it struck me that America is all about *more*. Italy is about quality—fish glistening with seawater, freshly laid eggs, just-picked fruits and vegetables. You could extend that idea of quality to the Italian way of life—living in a close-knit community, sharing what you have, and living as a person of quality, upholding community values and traditions.

America is about quantity—as much as you want of whatever you want, any time of year or even time of day. And socially, there's the same kind of quantity: a jumble of cultures, each with its own ideas, customs, standards, and tastes. There's no limit to the different traditions and values you might encounter in a single day.

So I decided to stay.

You see the mix of traditions in the cooking here. In Italy, there's a definite etiquette to preparing food: Certain cheeses don't mix, fish is cooked with garlic but not onions, fish and chicken would never be combined in a dish—so many rules. But in America, anything goes, and that can be a plus. I've come across ideas that really enhance Italian recipes, like cooking on a grill, which we don't do as much.

There are uniquely American foods that I've come to love, like ribs and spicy chicken wings. In Italy, we eat ribs, of course, but more delicately prepared, maybe roasted with garlic in the oven. But barbecued ribs—what a huge revelation! I think one of America's greatest gifts to the world is barbecue sauce.

STUFFED EGGPLANT PALERMO STYLE

MILINCIANE AMMUTTUNATE PALERMITANE

6 servings

ELVIRA PANTALEO ✳ Mint with cheese is a refreshing combination that's popular in Sicily. It's a lively stuffing for baby eggplants, which are then braised in tomato sauce.

8 ounces **caciocavallo**, shaved paper-thin with a cheese plane or a vegetable peeler
¼ cup packed fresh **mint**, chopped
½ teaspoon freshly ground **black pepper**
¼ teaspoon **salt**

6 baby Italian **eggplants** (4 ounces each)
3 **garlic** cloves, slivered
3 tablespoons **olive oil**
3 cups **sugo di pomodoro** (page 95) or **plain marinara sauce**

1. In a medium bowl, combine the caciocavallo, mint, pepper, and salt.

2. With a small sharp knife, make three parallel, equidistant cuts along the length of each eggplant from the rounded end to just below the stem, cutting about three-quarters into the vegetable without cutting all the way through. Fill these slits with the cheese mixture; slip the garlic into one of the slits in each eggplant. Don't overstuff; the eggplant needs to stay together as it cooks.

3. Warm the oil in a deep skillet set over medium heat. Add the eggplant, slit sides up, cover, and cook until the eggplant begins to soften, about 5 minutes.

4. Pour in the sugo; prod the eggplant with a rubber spatula to make sure they're not sticking. Cover, reduce the heat, and simmer until the eggplant is tender, about 15 minutes. Let cool in the pan for a few minutes before serving.

EGGPLANT WITH CHOCOLATE

MELANZANE ALLA CIOCCOLATA

 4 servings

NINA PICARIELLO ✳ Eggplant with chocolate is a little-known Italian specialty, a combination of sweet and sour, earthy and rich. With a dish this special, you should make your own tomato sauce. I do.

2 large Italian **eggplants** (about 12 ounces each), cut into ¼-inch-thick slices
1 tablespoon plus ¼ teaspoon **salt**
½ cup **olive oil**, or as needed
1 (28-ounce) can crushed **tomatoes**
6 tablespoons unsweetened **cocoa powder**

3 tablespoons **sugar**
¼ teaspoon ground **cinnamon**
¼ teaspoon freshly ground **black pepper**
Fresh **basil** leaves, for garnish
Extra-virgin **olive oil**, for garnish

1. Line your counter with paper towels; set a wire rack on top of them. Place the eggplant slices on the rack, sprinkle with 1 tablespoon of the salt on both sides, and let drain for 15 to 20 minutes. Rinse the slices and dry them well with fresh paper towels.

2. Meanwhile, warm 2 tablespoons of the oil in a medium saucepan set over medium heat. Add the tomatoes, cocoa powder, sugar, cinnamon, the ¼ teaspoon salt, and pepper. Bring to a brisk simmer, stirring often. Reduce the heat and simmer, stirring occasionally, until thick and rich, about 20 minutes.

3. As the sauce simmers, warm 2 tablespoons more oil in a large skillet set over medium heat. Slip several eggplant slices into the skillet without crowding and brown them on both sides, about 6 minutes, turning once. Drain the eggplant on paper towels and repeat with the remaining eggplant, working in batches, and adding more oil to the skillet as needed.

4. Divide the eggplant among four serving plates; ladle the sauce on top of and around the eggplant. Garnish with basil and extra-virgin olive oil.

◁ **NOTE** ▷ *You can also turn this into a casserole. Lightly oil a 9 x 13-inch baking pan with olive oil on a paper towel. Layer the fried eggplant in the pan, alternating with spoonfuls of the tomato-chocolate sauce. Bake until bubbling, about 20 minutes. Serve warm.*

CAPONATA CAPONATA

CHRISTINA NARISI CARROZZA ✳ This is my version of the classic Sicilian eggplant dish, which has been in my family for generations. During the summer, my whole family gathers to make a year's worth of tomato sauce, along with scores of jars of caponata.

1 head **celery** (about 1 pound), trimmed and thinly sliced
¾ cup **olive oil**, or as needed
5 large Italian **eggplants** (about 12 ounces each), cubed
2 medium **onions**, chopped (about 2 cups)
1½ cups canned **tomato puree**

¼ cup packed fresh **basil**, chopped
½ teaspoon **salt**
½ teaspoon freshly ground **black pepper**
2 cups **nonpareil capers** in brine, drained
1½ cups pitted **green olives**, thinly sliced
¼ cup **red wine vinegar**
¼ cup **sugar**

1. Bring a large pot of salted water to a boil. Add the celery, blanch for 1 minute, and drain.

2. Warm 2 tablespoons of the oil in a large skillet set over medium-high heat. Add as many eggplant cubes as possible without crowding the skillet; cook, turning occasionally, until golden on all sides, about 8 minutes. Transfer the eggplant to a large bowl, add more oil to the skillet, if needed, and continue browning further batches.

3. Add 2 tablespoons more oil to the skillet; then add the onions and cook, stirring often, until tender, about 8 minutes. Stir in the tomato puree, basil, salt, and pepper. Cook, stirring often, until the mixture has reduced by half, about 20 minutes.

4. Add the celery, eggplant, capers, olives, vinegar, and sugar. Return the mixture to a simmer, and cook until the eggplant is tender, about 30 minutes, stirring often and adding a little water as needed to keep the mixture from sticking. Remove from the heat. Let cool in the skillet until room temperature, about 1 hour; then cover and refrigerate for up to 4 days. Serve cold or at room temperature.

SICILIAN-STYLE STUFFED ARTICHOKES BRAISED IN TOMATO SAUCE CACUOCCIULI CU TAPPU

6 servings

ELVIRA PANTALEO ✳ In Sicily, we'd celebrate artichoke season with a big festival. My mother would put slivered garlic and salt and pepper between the leaves, then roast the artichokes. But stuffed and braised in tomato sauce, artichokes are even more delectable.

6 large **globe artichokes**
3 tablespoons fresh **lemon juice**
4 large **eggs**, at room temperature
¾ cup fresh **breadcrumbs**
½ cup packed fresh **flat-leaf parsley**, chopped
2 ounces **caciocavallo** or **Parmigiano-Reggiano**, finely grated (about ½ cup)
¼ cup **raisins**, chopped

¼ cup **pine nuts**, chopped
½ teaspoon **salt**
½ teaspoon freshly ground **black pepper**
2 tablespoons **canola** or **vegetable oil**
4 cups **sugo di pomodoro** (page 95) or plain **marinara sauce**
2 teaspoons **sugar**
Extra-virgin **olive oil**, for garnish

1. Cut off and discard the top third of each artichoke. Remove the tough outer leaves. Using your thumbs, gently pull apart the tender inner leaves to expose the center. Pull out and discard the prickly purple-tipped leaves and scoop out the fuzzy choke inside.

2. Trim the stems so the artichokes can sit flat. Fill a bowl with water and lemon juice, and add the artichokes. The artichokes can be set aside at room temperature for 3 hours.

3. Whisk 2 eggs in a large bowl until blended; stir in the breadcrumbs, parsley, caciocavallo, raisins, pine nuts, salt, and pepper. Stuff the artichokes with the mixture, pressing gently but firmly to compact the filling.

4. Beat the remaining 2 eggs in a shallow bowl. Heat a large skillet over medium heat and add the canola oil. Dip the stuffed side of each artichoke in the egg; set the artichoke in the skillet eggy side down to create a crust that seals the filling. Cook for 1 to 2 minutes, until just set. Gently turn the artichokes on all sides and brown lightly, about 5 minutes.

5. Set the artichokes egg side up in the skillet. Pour in the sugo; sprinkle with the sugar. Raise the heat to medium-high until the sugo starts to bubble, then cover, reduce the heat, and simmer until the artichokes are tender, about 20 minutes. Place the artichokes in bowls with some sugo and garnish with olive oil.

STUFFED ARTICHOKES CARCIOFI RIPIENI

 ──────────────────────────────── *4 servings* ┝━━━┥

CARMELINA PICA ✳ This is a traditional recipe for stuffed artichokes. Instead of a breadcrumb stuffing, the artichokes are stuffed with lots of garlic, parsley, and their own chopped stems.

4 large **globe artichokes**
¼ cup fresh **flat-leaf parsley**, minced
4 tablespoons **olive oil**

4 teaspoons minced **garlic**
¼ teaspoon **salt**
4 small pieces **Italian bread**

1. Cut off and discard the top quarter of each artichoke. Remove the tough outer leaves. Trim and discard the sharp points on the remaining leaves with kitchen shears. Slice off the stems so the artichokes can sit flat (do not discard the stems). Using your thumbs, gently pull apart the leaves until the center is exposed. Pull out and discard the prickly purple-tipped leaves. Using a spoon, scoop out and discard the fuzzy choke inside.

2. Peel and finely dice the reserved stems and place them in a medium bowl; stir in the parsley, oil, garlic, and salt. Divide this mixture evenly among the artichokes, filling their centers with the stuffing. Top the stuffing in each artichoke with a piece of bread cut to fit the opening.

3. Cut a piece of parchment paper to fit the inside of a large sauté pan or deep skillet, like a cover. Place the artichokes bread side up in the pan. Add enough water to come halfway up the sides of the artichokes. Set the pan over high heat and bring the water to a boil. Lay the piece of parchment paper over the artichokes (covering with a lid will soften the vegetables too much). Reduce the heat and simmer until tender, 45 to 55 minutes. Let cool for a few minutes before serving warm.

FRIED ARTICHOKES CARCIOFI FRITTI

4 servings

CHRISTINA NARISI CARROZZA ✳ In northern Italy, we loved to stick whole artichokes right into the fireplace to roast. Then we'd yank them out and shake them in a paper bag with olive oil, parsley, garlic, salt, and pepper. But a more elegant preparation is this especially light and delicious fried version.

4 large **globe artichokes**
Extra-virgin **olive oil**, for frying
4 large **eggs**, at room temperature

1 teaspoon **salt**, plus more for serving
1 teaspoon freshly ground **black pepper**

1. Bring a large pot of water to a rolling boil.

2. Cut off and discard the top half of each artichoke. Remove the outer leaves until you reach the tender inner leaves. Pull out and discard the prickly purple-tipped leaves. Using a spoon, scoop out and discard the fuzzy choke inside, revealing the heart. Cut each artichoke through the stem end into ½-inch-thick slices.

3. Add the artichokes to the pot and cook for 10 minutes. Drain and pat dry with paper towels.

4. Spread a layer of paper towels on a dry work surface and set a wire rack on top. Pour the oil into a deep skillet to a depth of 1 inch. Clip a deep-frying thermometer to the inside of the skillet and heat the oil over medium heat until it registers 325°F.

5. Whisk the eggs, salt, and pepper in a large bowl until well blended and creamy. Pat the artichokes dry once again. Dip one slice into the egg mixture, shake off the excess, and slip it into the hot oil. Repeat with as many artichoke slices as you can without crowding the skillet. Cook until golden brown, about 4 minutes, turning once. Transfer to the wire rack and continue frying more slices, adjusting the heat so the temperature of the oil remains constant. Season with salt before serving.

ARTICHOKE CAPONATA CAPONATA DI CARCIOFI

ELVIRA PANTALEO ✳ When people hear the word *caponata*, they assume that it refers to the eggplant version of this dish. But artichokes are just as wonderful in this classic sweet-and-sour preparation.

4 large **globe artichokes**
3 tablespoons fresh **lemon juice**
5 medium **celery** stalks, thinly sliced (about 2½ cups)
2 tablespoons **olive oil**
2 medium **onions**, halved and cut into thin half-moons
2 pounds **plum tomatoes**, peeled, cored, and chopped (see note)

1½ cups pitted **green olives**, chopped
1 cup dry **white wine**
3 tablespoons **nonpareil capers** in brine, drained
¼ cup **white wine vinegar**
2 tablespoons **sugar**
1 tablespoon **honey**
½ teaspoon **salt**
½ teaspoon freshly ground **black pepper**

1. Cut off and discard the top third of each artichoke. Remove the outer leaves until you reach the tender inner leaves. Carefully pull apart the leaves until the center is exposed. Pull out and discard the prickly purple-tipped leaves. Using a spoon, scoop out and discard the fuzzy choke inside. Quarter the artichokes and place them in a large bowl, cover with water, add the lemon juice, and stir well. (They can stand at room temperature for up to 3 hours.)

2. Bring a large saucepan of water to a boil. Add the celery and blanch for 1 minute. Drain well; leave the celery in the colander.

3. Warm the oil in a deep skillet set over medium heat. Add the onions and cook, stirring often, until golden brown, about 12 minutes. Stir in the tomatoes, olives, wine, and capers. Heat to a simmer, stirring often, until the tomatoes begin to break down, about 8 minutes.

4. Drain the artichokes over the celery, then add both to the skillet with the tomatoes. Stir in the vinegar, sugar, honey, salt, and pepper. Bring to a boil, then reduce the heat and cook, stirring often, until the sauce has thickened and the artichokes are tender, about 20 minutes. If the mixture becomes too dry, add warm water and reduce the heat. Although you can serve this dish immediately, it's better the next day after the flavors have blended.

◁ **NOTE** ▷ *To prepare the tomatoes, drop them into a large pot of boiling water and blanch for 2 minutes, just until their skins crack. Use a slotted spoon to transfer them to a large bowl of ice water, let cool completely, and then slip off their wrinkled skins.*

NEAPOLITAN POTATO PIE GATTÒ DI PATATE

CARMELINA PICA ✳ This is a traditional Neapolitan dish. I make it with russet potatoes and Parmigiano-Reggiano. Every family makes its own version of a classic like this.

10 tablespoons (1¼ sticks) unsalted **butter**, plus more for greasing

4 tablespoons Italian-style **breadcrumbs**

3 pounds russet **potatoes**, peeled and quartered

3 large **eggs**, well beaten

2 ounces **Parmigiano-Reggiano**, finely grated (about ½ cup)

8 ounces **ham**, cubed

4 ounces **salami**, casings removed and meat cubed

8 ounces **mozzarella**, shredded (about 2 cups)

½ cup packed fresh **flat-leaf parsley**, chopped

½ teaspoon **salt**

½ teaspoon freshly ground **black pepper**

1. Place the potatoes in a large saucepan, fill it three-quarters with water, and bring to a boil. Cook until tender, about 20 minutes. Drain well.

2. Position the rack in the center of the oven and preheat the oven to 375°F. Lightly butter a 9 x 13-inch baking dish and sprinkle it with 2 tablespoons of the breadcrumbs.

3. Pass the potatoes through a potato ricer into a large bowl, or mash them with a potato masher. Cut 8 tablespoons of the butter into small bits and add these while the potatoes are hot. Stir until the butter has melted.

4. Stir in the eggs, Parmigiano-Reggiano, ham, salami, mozzarella, parsley, salt, and pepper. Scoop the potato mixture into the baking dish and smooth the top; sprinkle with the remaining 2 tablespoons breadcrumbs. Cut the remaining 2 tablespoons butter into small bits and dot them across the top of the casserole.

5. Bake until the top is golden brown, about 20 minutes. Let cool on a wire rack for 10 minutes before serving.

SMOTHERED CAULIFLOWER CAVOLFIORE AFFOGATO

 4 servings

ELVIRA PANTALEO ✳ Cauliflower is a favorite vegetable in Sicily. It's often eaten with pasta. But I like to make it on its own, in this traditional style, in a skillet full of other vegetables and cheese.

1 large head **cauliflower** (about 2¼ pounds), cored and cut into florets
6 ounces **Pecorino Romano**, finely grated (about 1½ cups)
½ cup pitted **black olives**, finely chopped
4 **garlic** cloves
3 salt-packed **anchovies**, cleaned, deboned, rinsed, and finely chopped

1 medium fresh hot **red cherry pepper**, seeded and minced
¼ teaspoon freshly ground **black pepper**
3 tablespoons **olive oil**
½ cup dry **white wine**

1. Bring a large pot of water to a boil. Add the cauliflower and blanch just until the florets begin to soften, 2 to 3 minutes. Drain.

2. Transfer the florets to a large bowl. Stir in the Pecorino Romano, olives, garlic, anchovies, cherry pepper, and black pepper.

3. Warm the oil in a large nonstick skillet set over medium heat. Add the cauliflower mixture. Cook for 1 minute without stirring. Pour in the wine and reduce the heat to low. Cover and cook, stirring gently once in a while, for 10 minutes.

4. Uncover, raise the heat to medium, press the mixture down a bit, and continue cooking until all the liquid has evaporated and a crust begins to form on the bottom. Use a large, rubber spatula to flip sections of the mixture without stirring them too much. Continue cooking until browned and a little crusty on the other side, about 5 minutes. Discard the garlic cloves and spoon the cauliflower into a serving bowl.

BRAISED STUFFED ESCAROLE SCAROLA IMBOTTITA

4 servings

NINA PICARIELLO ✳ When I was growing up in my nonna's house, most of our vegetables came from her garden, including lots of escarole. I love to stuff the leaves with this flavorful mixture.

1 large head **escarole**, washed
4 tablespoons extra-virgin **olive oil**
2 tablespoons **pine nuts**, chopped
1 tablespoon **nonpareil capers** in brine, drained
2 **anchovy fillets**, chopped

1 teaspoon minced **garlic**
⅓ cup chopped pitted **black olives**
1 **plum tomato**, seeded and finely chopped
½ cup fresh **breadcrumbs**
1 cup **vegetable broth**

1. Set a large bowl of ice water next to the stove. Bring a large pot of water to a boil. Submerge the escarole in the boiling water, reduce the heat to medium, and cook for 2 minutes. Use tongs to transfer the escarole to the ice water. Submerge and cool.

2. Warm 2 tablespoons of the oil in a large skillet set over medium heat. Add the pine nuts, capers, anchovies, and garlic; cook until fragrant and lightly browned, stirring all the while, about 1 minute. Add the olives and tomato; cook for 1 minute. Stir in the breadcrumbs and scrape this mixture into a large bowl. Let cool for a few minutes.

3. Gently squeeze the escarole dry over the sink; set it on a cutting board. Carefully open the leaves and smear the breadcrumb mixture in the center of the head and between the larger leaves. Bring the leaves back into a fairly tight head. Tie gently but securely with butcher's twine to hold its shape.

4. In the same skillet, warm the remaining 2 tablespoons oil over medium heat. Set the stuffed escarole in the skillet and cook on all sides until lightly browned, turning occasionally with tongs, about 4 minutes.

5. Pour in the broth and reduce the heat to medium-low. Cover and cook until tender, 15 to 20 minutes, turning the head once or twice and basting it even more often with the broth. To serve, transfer the escarole to a cutting board; snip off the twine and cut the head into even quarters through its core. Serve warm, moistened with a little broth from the skillet, if desired.

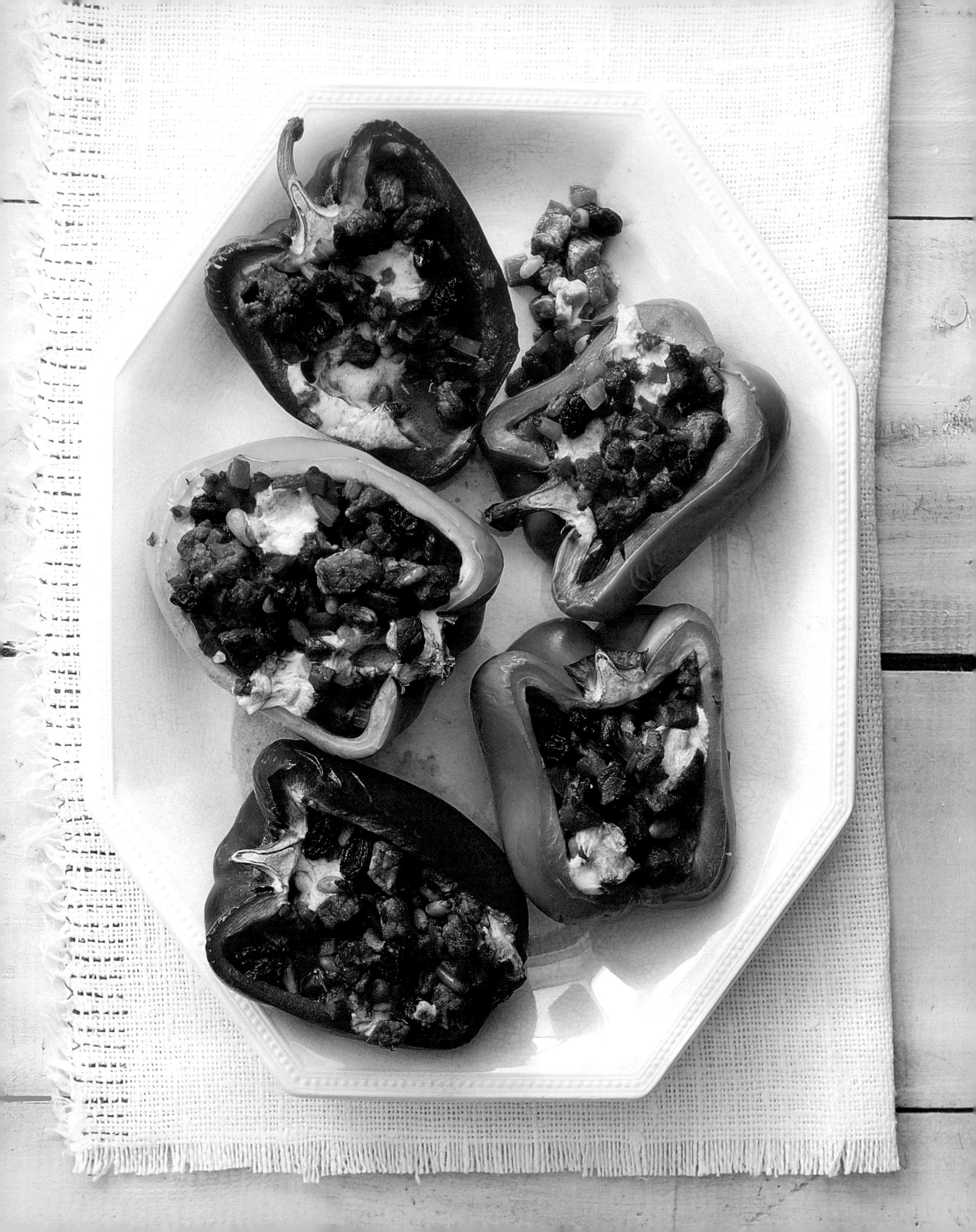

STUFFED PEPPERS with MEAT, PINE NUTS, AND RAISINS PEPERONI RIPIENI

 6 servings

MARGHERITA AMATO ✳ My stuffed peppers have both veal and pork, as well as lots of cheese, herbs, and spices. For a festive look, I like to use red, orange, and yellow bell peppers.

½ cup **olive oil**
1 small **onion**, chopped (about ½ cup)
1 medium **carrot**, chopped (about ½ cup)
1 medium **celery** stalk, chopped (about ½ cup)
8 ounces **ground veal**
8 ounces **ground pork**
1 cup dry **white wine**
1 cup **sugo di pomodoro** (page 95) or plain marinara sauce
3½ ounces **mozzarella**, diced
2 tablespoons **pine nuts**

2 tablespoons **raisins**
2 tablespoons minced fresh **flat-leaf parsley**
1 teaspoon minced **garlic**
½ teaspoon **salt**
½ teaspoon freshly ground **black pepper**
6 large **bell peppers**, preferably 2 red, 2 yellow, and 2 orange, halved lengthwise and seeded
Finely grated **Grana Padano**, for garnish (optional)

1. Warm the oil in a large skillet set over medium heat. Add the onion, carrot, and celery. Cook, stirring occasionally, until the vegetables are golden brown, about 10 minutes.

2. Crumble in the ground veal and pork; cook, stirring often, until lightly browned, about 10 minutes. Pour in the wine and bring to a boil over medium-high heat. Cook, stirring occasionally, until about half the wine has been absorbed. Remove from the heat and let cool to room temperature, about 1 hour.

3. Meanwhile, position the rack in the center of the oven and preheat the oven to 350°F.

4. Stir the sugo, mozzarella, pine nuts, raisins, parsley, garlic, salt, and black pepper into the meat mixture.

5. Set the bell peppers cut side up on a large rimmed baking sheet. Spoon the meat mixture into the bell peppers, gently packing it into place. Bake until the mozzarella has melted and the bell peppers are tender, about 20 minutes. Let cool a few minutes before serving warm. Sprinkle with Grana Padano when serving, if desired.

ROASTED RED PEPPERS with BREADCRUMBS AND OLIVES PEPERONI ARROSTITI

6 servings

CARMELINA PICA ✳ Years ago, I concocted this side dish of roasted red pepper strips. It soon became one of the biggest hits in the appetizer section of my brother-in-law's Italian food market on Staten Island.

6 large red **bell peppers**, seeded and cut into 1-inch-wide strips
4 tablespoons **olive oil**
¼ cup **nonpareil capers** in brine, drained
¼ cup pitted **black olives**, preferably Gaeta, chopped
¼ cup **pine nuts**
2 teaspoons minced **garlic**
¼ teaspoon **salt**
¼ teaspoon freshly ground **black pepper**
1 cup Italian-style **breadcrumbs**

1. Position the rack in the center of the oven and preheat the oven to 350°F.

2. Toss the bell peppers with the oil, capers, olives, pine nuts, garlic, salt, and black pepper in a large roasting pan. Bake for 45 minutes, tossing every 15 minutes.

3. Add the breadcrumbs and toss well. Continue baking until the breadcrumbs are crunchy and the bell peppers are soft, 10 to 15 minutes. Let cool for 10 minutes to serve warm, or cool to room temperature before serving.

STUFFED FRIED CARDOONS CARDI RIPIENI E FRITTI

 4 to 6 servings

CHRISTINA NARISI CARROZZA ✳ Cardoons are vegetables especially beloved in Sicily. They are served on holidays like Christmas, New Year's Eve, and Easter. They taste like artichokes but they're easier to eat, without the hard outer leaves.

2 pounds **cardoons**, trimmed, stalks cut into 6-inch lengths
3 medium **lemons**, halved
4 tablespoons **olive oil**, plus more as needed
1½ tablespoons minced **garlic**
5 **anchovy fillets**, minced

1½ cups fresh **breadcrumbs**
¼ cup packed fresh **flat-leaf parsley**, minced
2 ounces **Pecorino Romano,** finely grated (about ½ cup)
4 large **eggs**, at room temperature
½ teaspoon **salt**

1. Bring a large pot of water to a boil. Add the cardoons and the lemon halves. Boil until the cardoons are tender, 20 to 30 minutes. Drain and discard the lemons. Let cool to room temperature, about 30 minutes.

2. Meanwhile, warm the oil in a medium skillet set over medium heat. Add the garlic and anchovies; cook, stirring continuously, until fragrant, about 20 seconds. Stir in the bread-crumbs, parsley, and Pecorino Romano. Cook until the breadcrumbs are lightly toasted, stirring often and adding more oil if the mixture appears dry. Remove from the heat and let cool to room temperature, about 30 minutes.

3. To stuff the cardoons, lay the cardoon stalks on a cutting board and slice them length-wise about three-quarters of the way through so that they can be opened like a book. Stuff each cardoon with about 2 tablespoons of the breadcrumb mixture, fold, and tie shut in two places with butcher's twine.

4. Spread a layer of paper towels on a dry work surface and set a wire rack on top. Pour oil into a large skillet to a depth of 1 inch. Clip a deep-frying thermometer to the inside of the skillet and heat the oil over medium heat until the temperature registers 325°F.

5. Whisk the eggs and salt in a bowl until uniform. Dip a stuffed cardoon into the eggs and then slip it into the oil. Repeat with 4 or 5 more stuffed cardoons, without crowding the skillet; fry until golden brown, turning once, about 4 minutes. Using a slotted spoon, transfer the fried cardoons to the wire rack to drain, and continue frying more cardoon bundles. Let cool for 10 minutes to serve warm, or cool to room temperature.

FENNEL WITH GORGONZOLA

FINOCCHIO AL GORGONZOLA

 4 to 6 servings

ROSA TURANO ✳ Braised fennel is made even more tempting with Gorgonzola in my recipe for this classic side dish. Add just enough broth so the fennel gets tender without becoming soupy.

3 tablespoons unsalted **butter**
3 tablespoons **olive oil**
1 medium **onion**, finely chopped (about 1 cup)
2 large **fennel bulbs**, trimmed, halved, cored, and thinly sliced
¼ teaspoon **salt**

¼ teaspoon freshly ground **black pepper**
½ cup **chicken broth**, or as needed
4 ounces **Gorgonzola**, crumbled (about 1 cup)
1 ounce **Parmigiano-Reggiano**, finely grated (about ¼ cup; optional)

1. Melt the butter in the oil in a large skillet set over medium heat. Add the onion and cook, stirring often, until softened, about 4 minutes.

2. Add the fennel, salt, and pepper. Cook, stirring often, for 5 minutes. Add 2 tablespoons of the broth and continue cooking, stirring often, and adding more broth every few minutes, until the fennel is tender, about 15 minutes.

3. When the broth has been absorbed and the fennel is tender, turn off the heat and sprinkle with the Gorgonzola. Cover and set aside for 5 minutes so that the cheese melts. If desired, and if you've used a broiler-safe pan, dust the dish with Parmigiano-Reggiano, set the skillet 4 to 6 inches from a heated broiler, and broil until lightly brown, 1 to 2 minutes.

VEGETABLE FRITTERS WITH TWO BATTERS

VERDURE FRITTE CON DUE PASTELLE

 6 to 8 servings per batter

ADELINA ORAZZO ✳ These batters add a big dimension of flavor to vegetables prepared *fritto misto* style. Use either batter or make both at the same meal.

FOR THE BEER BATTER
1½ cups **all-purpose flour**
½ teaspoon **salt**
¼ teaspoon freshly ground **black pepper**

2 large **eggs**
2 cups light-colored **beer**, such as Moretti or Peroni

FOR THE CHICKPEA BATTER
2¾ cups **chickpea flour**
1 teaspoon active dry **yeast**
½ teaspoon **salt**

½ teaspoon freshly ground **black pepper**
2 cups plain **seltzer**

FRESH VEGETABLES FOR EACH BATTER
2 medium **onions**, cut into ½-inch-wide slices and separated into rings
3 medium **zucchini**, cut into ½-inch-thick slices

2 cups **broccoli** florets (about 2 inches each)
2 cups **cauliflower** florets (about 2 inches each)

Canola or **vegetable oil**, for frying
Salt, preferably coarse or flaked

1. To make the beer batter, sift the flour into a medium bowl, then stir in the salt and pepper. Using a wooden spoon, stir in the eggs until the batter begins to get thick and pasty. Then using a whisk, stir in the beer in a slow, steady stream, whisking continuously to avoid clumps, until smooth. Set aside for 30 minutes at room temperature.

2. To make the chickpea batter, mix the chickpea flour, yeast, salt, and pepper in a medium bowl. Using a whisk, add the seltzer a little at a time, whisking continuously to avoid clumps, until smooth. Set aside at room temperature for 20 minutes.

3. Spread a layer of paper towels on a dry work surface and set a wire rack on top. Dry the vegetables well with paper towels. For either batter, pour oil into a large saucepan or Dutch oven to a depth of 3 inches. Clip a deep-frying thermometer to the inside of the pan and heat the oil over medium-high heat until the temperature registers 325°F.

4. Dip the vegetables one piece at a time in the preferred batter. Slip into the oil and repeat with six to eight more pieces, just enough so the pan is not crowded. Adjust the heat to keep the oil's temperature constant. Fry, turning occasionally, until golden brown, 3 to 4 minutes. Use a slotted spoon to transfer the vegetables to the wire rack. Sprinkle with salt while hot. Continue frying more vegetables, then serve on a big platter.

VEGETABLE RICOTTA CUPS COPPE DI RICOTTA

 8 servings

NINA PICARIELLO ✳ This is the kind of dish we'd make with the bounty of my nonna's garden. I cut the vegetables matchstick size, then bake them in a cheesy custard sauce.

2 medium **carrots**, julienned

2 small **zucchini**, julienned

1 medium yellow **potato**, peeled and julienned

4 tablespoons (½ stick) unsalted **butter**, plus more for the custard cups

1 cup whole **milk**

3 tablespoons **all-purpose flour**

1 cup whole-milk **ricotta**

2 ounces finely grated **Pecorino Romano** (about ½ cup)

½ teaspoon **salt**

¼ teaspoon freshly ground **black pepper**

1 large **egg** plus 1 large **egg yolk**, at room temperature

2 cups **vegetable broth**

½ pound fresh shelled **peas** or thawed frozen

1. Bring a large saucepan of water to a boil. Add the carrots, zucchini, and potato and cook until very soft, about 5 minutes. Drain well—excess water will ruin the custards.

2. Position the rack in the center of the oven and preheat the oven to 325°F. Generously butter eight 1-cup custard cups or ramekins.

3. Warm the milk in a small saucepan over low heat without bubbling.

4. Melt the 4 tablespoons butter in a medium saucepan set over medium-low heat. Whisk in the flour until pasty, then gradually whisk in the warmed milk. Cook, whisking continuously, for 5 minutes, until thickened and bubbling.

5. Whisk in the ricotta, Pecorino Romano, salt, and pepper until smooth. Remove the pan from the heat just before the sauce returns to a boil.

6. Whisk the egg and egg yolk in a large bowl until smooth. Slowly whisk in the hot ricotta mixture until well blended.

7. Divide the vegetables among the custard cups. Top each with the ricotta sauce. Set the custard cups on a rimmed baking sheet. Bake until the custard is set, about 20 minutes.

8. Meanwhile, in a medium saucepan, bring the broth to a boil. Add the peas and cook until tender, about 3 minutes. Drain the peas, reserving the broth.

9. Place the peas in a food processor or blender. Cover and process until smooth, adding the reserved broth 1 or 2 tablespoons at a time until the mixture has the consistency of a puree.

10. To serve, set each custard cup on a plate and top with some of the pea puree.

V

CEREALI, RISO e GNOCCHI

JODY SCARAVELLA *My father comes from Piacenza in northern Italy, which has food traditions completely different from those of my Sicilian grandmother. Through the nonnas at the Enoteca, I've come to love dishes more typical of the north, like farro, risotto, and polenta. But of course my heart lies with the dishes I grew up on, like Nonna Domenica's gnocchi— little puffs of happiness—which she rolled off a fork to create the perfect grooves for catching sauce.*

Rosa Turano

I'm from Schio, a town in the Vicenza province of Veneto, a region of northern Italy. Jody always wants us to cook super-authentic, super-ethnic dishes, like we make at home, not restaurant food. So, for New Year's Eve, he asked me, "Can you make *cotechino*?"

Me in Italy in the 1960s

Cotechino is a sausage you have to boil for hours; there are many types in Veneto. But what Jody meant was cotechino with *lenticchie* (lentils), which we eat on New Year's Eve to bring us luck and money in the year ahead.

"Sure," I said. That night, I soaked some dried chestnuts to take with me to the restaurant. The next day, I cooked them for a good hour and combined them with the lentils made my usual way, with the holy trinity of onion, carrots, and celery. I cook the cotechino and lay it on top of the lentils to keep warm. That's how I planned to serve it for New Year's Eve dinner. In northern Italy, though, we'd round out the dish with some mashed potatoes and sauerkraut.

But wouldn't you know it, hardly any of the guests even noticed the cotechino on the menu. So I asked Jody, "Now what I am supposed to do?"

He told me, "At midnight, bring out a little dish for everyone. Let them taste it, and maybe it will make their year."

So I did, and everyone loved it—both the dish and the tradition. The leftovers I took home for New Year's Day breakfast with my husband.

Schio has grown to be almost a big city, instead of my little, half-rural hometown. The fields are gone, and the cemetery has gotten so crowded that if you're willing to be cremated, the state will pay for your burial.

Schio is an age-old center for textiles. My father was an administrator at Lanerossi, a top weaving factory, but he always had the bug for America. So in 1955, he got someone to guarantee him a job in Union City, America's Embroidery Capital. He went from an executive job in Italy to working embroidery machines, double shifts, so he could bring us over.

I arrived in New York with my mother and two sisters on July 3, 1956. We came over on the *Andrea Doria*. On its very next ocean crossing, the ship was traveling in heavy fog when another liner crashed into it. We lived in an apartment in Weehawken, New Jersey, with a view of New York Harbor. We went down to watch "our" ship come in, but it never did. When we got home, my mother told us, "Ohhh! The ship has sunk!" That was scary.

I was fourteen years old, so I had to go to school, though my sisters and I spoke very little English. They made an announcement over the loudspeaker, asking kids who spoke Italian to come to the office to help us. All these Sicilians and Neapolitans showed up, but their southern dialects were even stranger to me than English. I'd never heard those dialects and wouldn't understand them until later, when I married a Sicilian.

The school put me in classes where language wouldn't matter, like music appreciation and sewing. In cooking class, they taught me to make pineapple upside-down cake—I mean, really. By then I already knew how to cook from observing my nonna, who was well known in Schio for her food and hospitality.

Since my mother worked, my sisters and I hung out at my nonna's house, helping in the kitchen and garden. We'd pick wild strawberries in the fields, which my nonna taught us to clean. The whole time we worked, she'd make us whistle—seriously!—to be sure we weren't gobbling them up. It was worth waiting to enjoy the strawberries with cream that she whipped with her wicker whisk. Nearly every tool in her kitchen, in her household, was homemade.

She was a perfectionist, a strict homemaker, with beds made just so and the laundry unfailingly done by hand and hung out to dry on Mondays. In the kitchen, especially, she was a stickler. That may have been one reason why, as my mother used to say, cooking skipped a generation in our family.

I was the one who inherited my nonna's love of cooking. Entertaining, to me, is second nature. My husband, Jack, who built a business importing furniture from Italy, had a showroom in High Point, North Carolina. Every April and October, all the buyers would come down for the big furniture shows. To attract them to our place, I'd whip

My son at my grandparents' house, 1973

up a lavish dinner buffet. Sometimes, buyers would call to ask, joking, "Can I make a reservation?"

At first I served my usual northern Italian fare. But then people started asking for eggplant or chicken Parmesan, spaghetti with big meatballs, and baked ziti—dishes that, to me, were a mishmash. "Ma, you've got to cook Italian American food," my son told me, "or otherwise they won't eat."

So I learned and came up with some crowd-pleasers. But I would never serve those dishes in my home.

I love to cook the way my nonna did, with butter and cream. My husband has diabetes and other problems, so at home I have to keep things simple—lots of grilling and broiling. But at the Enoteca, I cut loose. Some of my pasta sauces might not be ones that you'd want to eat every day, but they're a great treat—say, if you're out to dinner at a restaurant.

One is a Gorgonzola sauce that I serve on farfalle, the bow tie pasta. It's very simple. I melt butter, then drop in pieces of Gorgonzola, melt those, and add heavy cream. In Italy they use an even richer cream called *panna*. I love to make a sauce like this with cauliflower, too. You just steam or boil the cauliflower, then chop it and sauté it in the butter before adding the Gorgonzola. I add a little tomato sauce at the end to give it a nice pink tinge, then finish off the sauce with Parmesan. Heaven!

I also use cream in a sauce with shrimp for penne or other sturdy pasta. I sauté shrimp in butter until it's pink, which happens quickly. Then I take it out and chop it—not too finely, but you don't want to get big chunks of it in the pasta—and set it aside. Next, I sauté onions and garlic in the same pan, adding a few fresh tomatoes (canned ones are fine), clam juice, a splash of white wine, and a little chicken stock. When the mixture concentrates, I toss in lots of chopped parsley and basil; and when I'm almost ready to serve it, I put the shrimp back in for a minute or two to absorb the flavors. Finally, I add a good dollop of heavy cream. I pour the sauce over the cooked pasta, dust it with Parmesan—yes, you can add cheese to a fish dish—and more chopped parsley and basil.

So easy, but so luxurious.

Today, people worry not only about fats but also about carbohydrates. So it might seem strange that in Italy, it's traditional to eat pasta with potatoes. That's a dish even my mother, who hated cooking, used to make.

What I do is cube celery, onions, and carrots and sauté them in butter, with garlic. As the mixture starts to brown, I throw in cubed raw potatoes and maybe some cubes of pancetta. Then I add whatever stock I have—chicken or beef or vegetable—and crushed tomatoes. I cook the sauce, covered, till the potatoes are tender, and serve it over pasta with lots of Parmesan. The sauce tastes even better the next day.

As a child, I learned to make gnocchi with potatoes. There are different kinds of gnocchi—some made with flour and breadcrumbs, some with ricotta—but my nonna belonged to the potato school. She'd start by using russet or baking potatoes, boil and mash them, then mix them with flour—without eggs, which some people use, but they can make the gnocchi heavy—and roll the dough in the shape of a long, thin tube. Then she'd go, "Ti-ti-ti-ti-ti-ti . . ." cutting the roll of dough by hand into small pieces. I'd love to gather them and line them up, not touching—as she insisted—so they'd stay separate when dropped into boiling water.

The gnocchi sauce my grandkids love is very rich. I mix creamy Gorgonzola, mascarpone, and grated asiago cheese, thinning them with heavy cream. Then I pour the sauce over the gnocchi and bake them until a nice crust forms. You can use the same sauce with tortellini. It's always a hit.

Rice dishes are popular in northern Italy, especially risotto. People find risotto intimidating, but it's super easy. The basic recipe is to sauté finely chopped onions or shallots in butter, lightly toast the rice in the fat, add white wine and let it evaporate, then stir in cupfuls of simmering chicken stock. Ingredients that need to be sautéed, like garlic or soaked porcini, should go in before the rice; for porcini, I'd use beef stock and add the soaking liquid. Ingredients like fresh asparagus or peas—as in the classic dish from my region dish *risi e bisi* (rice and peas)—would go in at the stock stage. The rice is done when it's still a bit moist—what we call *all'onda*, which means "on the wave." That's all there is to it.

One of the nonnas taught me a trick to use if you don't feel like standing and stirring your risotto for twenty minutes straight. After you add stock for ten minutes, and it's been absorbed, you lay out the rice on a flat platter to cool. Later, you can return it to the pot and simply stir and add stock until it's done.

Then you take the risotto off the heat, add plenty of butter and cheese, and enjoy!

My region of Italy, Veneto, is particularly famous for its polenta. My Sicilian husband calls me the *polentona* because we northern Italians eat so much of it. But from the first time I served polenta, he loved it and he actually brags about how good mine is.

I learned to make it from my nonna, who was a polenta purist. It had to be made in a copper pot, with just water and salt, and stirred continuously. Of course, there was no such thing as instant polenta back then.

My nonna loved her polenta really soft, like thick porridge. My grandfather liked his nice and hard, so you could slice it. She would alternate, making it hard one time and soft the next. When she made it soft and turned it out of the pot, onto a wooden board, my grandfather would always say, "Close the door! Nonna's pouring the polenta. It's going to run away!"

When she made polenta for my grandfather, my nonna would cut off a good slice—the traditional way to slice polenta is using a piece of thread—and grill it in her fireplace. Then she'd serve it *all'uccellino,* meaning topped with "little birds."

That was the classic combination in my region. There was a hut sitting in the middle of the fields where guys with pellet guns would hang out and shoot all these tiny, tiny birds. My nonna would run them onto a skewer and roast them over the coals, then we'd eat the whole bird, bones and all. The head was the best part.

When I told my family this story, one of my sons said, "How cruel! How could you eat them?" My husband said, "You were a cannibal!"

But is it really so different from eating anything else, like a chicken? Or a quail? I guess those birds were endangered or something because you can't eat them in Italy anymore. Shooting them is illegal.

In the restaurant, I serve polenta with rabbit, which is a very typical of my region.

But I'm not as much of a purist as my nonna. I add something extra to my rabbit now—mushrooms, to deepen the flavor. And when making polenta, I stir in some mascarpone, which makes it so rich and creamy. I add it right at the beginning so it gets incorporated during cooking. My nonna would be shocked, I'm sure. But food is always changing. It's not abandoning tradition to improve things.

CLASSIC POLENTA POLENTA CLASSICA

6 servings

ROSA TURANO ✳ This is the way my nonna made polenta—pure, with just water and salt.

1 teaspoon **salt**
1 cup medium- or coarse-ground yellow
  cornmeal or **polenta**

1. Bring 4 cups water and the salt to a boil in a large saucepan. Whisk in the cornmeal in a thin, steady stream.

2. Reduce the heat to medium and whisk for 2 minutes.

3. Reduce the heat to very low and cook at the barest bubble, stirring every 3 minutes with a wooden spoon, until thick, about 45 minutes. Serve hot, or pour into a 9 x 13-inch baking dish and let cool for 10 to 20 minutes to continue thickening.

POLENTA with DRIED FISH and CAULIFLOWER

POLENTA CON STOCCO E CAVOLFIORE

 ———————————————————————————————— *4 servings* ⊢——⊣

FRANCESCA LEONE ✳ *Stocco* is air-dried fish—cod, or sometimes haddock or pollock—that's not salted (as opposed to the more familiar dried, salted cod or *baccalà*).

1 pound **stocco**
1 small head **cauliflower** (about 1¼ pounds), cored and cut into 1-inch florets
2 medium **onions**, chopped (about 2 cups)
5 tablespoons **olive oil**
¼ cup finely chopped **fennel fronds**
1 medium fresh hot **red cherry pepper**, seeded and minced

1 cup **tomato puree**
2 tablespoons minced fresh **flat-leaf parsley**
1 **bay leaf**
1 teaspoon **salt**
½ teaspoon freshly ground **black pepper**
1¼ cups medium- or coarse-ground yellow **cornmeal** or **polenta**

1. Submerge the stocco in a large bowl of fresh water. Refrigerate for 3 to 4 days, changing the water daily. The fish must double in size and weight. Drain well.

2. In a medium saucepan, combine the cauliflower with 1 cup of the onions, 3 tablespoons of the oil, and 1 cup water. Bring to a simmer over medium heat, then cook until the cauliflower is al dente, no more than 5 minutes. Drain well.

3. Warm the remaining 2 tablespoons oil in a deep skillet set over medium heat. Add the remaining 1 cup onions, the fennel, and cherry pepper. Cook for 1 minute, stirring often, then reduce the heat to low and slip the stocco into the skillet. Cook for about 10 minutes, turning once. Transfer the stocco to a large cutting board.

4. Add the tomato puree, parsley, and bay leaf to the skillet. Simmer, stirring occasionally, for 5 minutes.

5. Meanwhile, debone the fish and cut the meat into 2-inch squares. Add them to the sauce and cook for 10 minutes. Stir in the cauliflower mixture, salt, and black pepper; cover and remove from the heat. Remove and discard the bay leaf.

6. In a large pot, bring 5 cups water to a boil. Stir in the cornmeal in a slow, steady stream. Cook, stirring continuously, until thick and uniform, about 15 minutes.

7. Add the stocco and the cauliflower mixture, stirring very gently with a wooden spoon to avoid breaking up the fish, simmer for a minute or two to warm through before serving.

RICE BALLS with PORK and SAFFRON

ARANCINI CON PORCO E ZAFFERANO

 8 servings

MARGHERITA AMATO ✳ Rice balls are one of our traditional foods for St. Lucy's Day, when we don't eat anything with yeast. I like to serve them the rest of the year, too, especially when one of my grandsons insists that his Nonnina—not his mother or his aunt—make him a batch.

6 cups **vegetable broth**
¼ teaspoon **saffron**
2½ cups **arborio rice**
2 tablespoons unsalted **butter**
½ ounce **Grana Padano**, finely grated (about 2 tablespoons)
4 tablespoons **olive oil**
1 small **onion**, chopped (about ½ cup)
1 small **carrot**, diced (about ¼ cup)

1 medium **celery** stalk, chopped (about ½ cup)
5 ounces **ground pork**
½ cup frozen **peas**, thawed
¼ cup **tomato paste**
¼ cup dry **white wine**
3 cups fresh **breadcrumbs**
Canola or **vegetable oil**, for frying

1. Combine the broth and saffron in a large saucepan; bring to a boil. Stir in the rice, then reduce the heat and simmer, stirring occasionally, until the rice is tender and all the broth has been absorbed. Remove from the heat; stir in the butter and Grana Padano until melted. Let cool to room temperature, about 2 hours.

2. Meanwhile, warm the olive oil in a large skillet set over medium heat. Add the onion, carrot, and celery; cook, stirring often, until the onion is lightly browned, about 10 minutes.

3. Crumble in the ground pork and cook, stirring frequently, until lightly browned, about 4 minutes. Add the peas and tomato paste; stir until well combined. Pour in the wine, reduce the heat to low, and cook, stirring often, until bubbling and very thick, about 5 minutes. Remove from the heat and let cool to room temperature, about 1 hour.

4. Spread the breadcrumbs on a plate. With wet hands, scoop up about 2½ tablespoons of the cooked rice and flatten it in your palms. Place 2 teaspoons of the meat filling in the center, then enclose the filling in the rice and form the rice into a ball, sealing it well. Roll the ball in the breadcrumbs, shaking off any excess, then set it aside and continue filling and forming rice balls until all the rice has been used, wetting your hands frequently so the rice doesn't stick. You'll make about 32 rice balls.

5. Line a large baking sheet with paper towels. Pour the canola oil into a large pot or Dutch oven to a depth of 3 inches. Clip a deep-frying thermometer to the inside of the pot and heat the oil over medium heat until it registers 325°F. Add six or eight balls to the hot oil, without crowding, and fry until golden, turning occasionally with a slotted spoon, about 4 minutes. Transfer to the baking sheet to drain and continue frying more rice balls, adjusting the heat to keep the oil's temperature constant. Serve hot.

RISOTTO WITH RADICCHIO RISOTTO CON RADICCHIO

 ——— *4 to 6 servings* ⊢——⊣

ROSA TURANO ✳ My region, Veneto, is famous for radicchio, sometimes called Italian chicory. Not only is it delicious, it's also an ancient folk cure for insomnia, among other ailments.

4 cups **chicken broth**, preferably homemade
6 tablespoons (¾ stick) unsalted **butter**
1 large **onion**, chopped (about 1½ cups)
1½ cups white **arborio** or **Carnaroli rice**

¾ cup dry **white wine**
1 small head **radicchio** (about 8 ounces), cored and chopped
Finely grated **Parmigiano-Reggiano**, for garnish

1. Heat the broth in a medium saucepan and keep it warm, but not boiling, as you make the risotto.

2. In a large sauté pan or a risotto pan, melt 2 tablespoons of the butter over medium heat. Add the onion and cook until softened, stirring often, about 4 minutes. Do not brown the onion.

3. Stir in the rice and cook until it begins to crackle or stick, about 2 minutes. Pour in the wine and bring to a brisk simmer. When the wine has been absorbed, stir in the radicchio.

4. Pour in 1 cup of the warm broth, reduce the heat to low, and stir continuously until the broth has been almost fully absorbed. It should take about 5 minutes. If not, your heat is too high or too low. Continue adding more broth, about ½ cup at a time, stirring each time until the stock is fully absorbed before adding more and reserving ½ cup broth for the end after the rice is tender—which will happen in about 20 minutes.

5. Stir in the final ½ cup broth and the remaining 4 tablespoons butter until melted. Serve with Parmigiano-Reggiano on top.

BUTTERNUT SQUASH RISOTTO

RISOTTO DI ZUCCA

 6 servings

CHRISTINA NARISI CARROZZA ✳ Because butternut squash can be stored for months, this is a winter dish in northern Italy. Try it on a chilly night. It's one of my vegetable-loving daughter's favorites.

1 large **butternut squash** (about 1½ pounds), halved lengthwise and seeded
4 tablespoons **olive oil**
2 fresh **sage** leaves, plus more for garnish
3 cups **vegetable broth**
3 tablespoons unsalted **butter**

1 medium **onion**, chopped (about 1 cup)
2 cups **arborio** or **Carnaroli rice**
1 cup dry **white wine**
½ teaspoon **salt**
½ teaspoon freshly ground **black pepper**
Finely grated **Parmigiano-Reggiano**, for garnish

1. Position the rack in the center of the oven and preheat the oven to 375°F.

2. Place the squash cut side up on a large, rimmed baking sheet. Drizzle each half with 1 tablespoon of the oil and tuck a sage leaf into each cavity. Bake until tender when pierced with a fork, about 40 minutes. Remove from the oven and set aside until cool enough to handle, about 20 minutes.

3. Use a large serving spoon to scoop and scrape the butternut squash out of its peel, discarding the sage leaf. Discard the peel and coarsely chop the squash.

4. Heat the broth in a medium saucepan over medium-high heat until hot but not bubbling. Reduce the heat to very low and keep warm while you prepare the risotto.

5. In a large sauté pan, melt the butter in the remaining 2 tablespoons oil over medium heat. Add the onion and cook, stirring often, until translucent, about 4 minutes. Add the rice and cook, stirring occasionally, until golden brown, about 4 minutes.

6. Pour in the wine, reduce the heat to low, and cook, stirring continously, until the wine has been absorbed, about 3 minutes. Stir in the salt and pepper.

7. Begin adding the warm broth, about ½ cup at a time, stirring continuously until each addition has been absorbed before adding the next. Continue cooking, stirring and adding more broth, until the rice is tender, about 20 minutes. Stir in the squash. Serve with Parmigiano-Reggiano and a few sage leaves sprinkled over the top.

RISOTTO WITH STRAWBERRIES

RISOTTO ALLE FRAGOLE

6 servings

CHRISTINA NARISI CARROZZA ✳ This risotto was inspired by an Italian combination I love: pears with Parmesan cheese. It struck me that the tang of strawberries would make a nice counterpoint to the creaminess of the risotto and the nuttiness of the cheese. Nice and light, it's a perfect dish for summer, like a warm-weather version of my butternut squash risotto. Don't even think about using frozen strawberries!

3 cups **vegetable broth**
3 tablespoons unsalted **butter**
3 tablespoons **olive oil**
1 medium **onion**, chopped (about 1 cup)
2 cups **arborio** or **Carnaroli rice**
1 cup moderately dry **white wine**

½ teaspoon **salt**
½ teaspoon freshly ground **black pepper**
3 cups sliced hulled **strawberries** (about
  10 ounces)
1 ounce **Parmigiano-Reggiano**, finely
  grated (about ¼ cup)

1. Heat the broth in a medium saucepan over medium-high heat until hot but not boiling. Reduce the heat to low and keep warm while you prepare the risotto.

2. Melt the butter with the oil in a large sauté pan set over medium heat. Add the onion and cook, stirring often, until translucent, about 4 minutes. Stir in the rice and cook, stirring continuously, for 1 minute, until the rice is coated in the butter and oil. Do not let the rice or onion brown.

3. Pour in the wine and stir well. Reduce the heat to low and simmer, stirring continuously, until the wine has been absorbed. Stir in the salt and pepper.

4. Reduce the heat to very low and start adding the broth ½ cup at a time, stirring continuously after each addition until the broth has been absorbed before adding the next. Continue cooking, adding broth and stirring all the while, until all the broth has been used and the rice is tender, about 20 minutes. Remove from the heat and divide among the serving bowls. Sprinkle the strawberries and Parmigiano-Reggiano on top so the cheese melts a bit from the heat of the rice.

RISOTTO WITH ARTICHOKES AND SHRIMP

RISOTTO CON CARCIOFI E GAMBERI

 4 to 6 servings

CARMELINA PICA ✳ This dish is light and elegant. Look for good-quality fish broth in the freezer section of gourmet supermarkets or at Italian markets.

2 large **globe artichokes**, or 1 (9-ounce) box frozen **artichoke hearts**, thawed
3 tablespoons **lemon juice**
3 tablespoons extra-virgin **olive oil**, plus more for garnish
1 teaspoon minced **garlic**
½ pound medium **shrimp** (about 30 per pound), peeled, deveined, and halved

2 medium **plum tomatoes**, chopped
½ teaspoon **salt**
6 cups **fish broth**
¼ cup chopped **onion**
3 cups **arborio** or **Carnaroli rice**
1 cup dry **white wine**

1. Cut off and discard the top half of each artichoke as well as the stem. Remove the outer leaves, then gently open the tender, inner leaves. Pull out and discard the prickly purple-tipped leaves. Using a spoon, scoop out and discard the fuzzy choke. Cut the artichokes into quarters, drop them into a bowl of water, and stir in the lemon juice.

2. Warm 1 tablespoon of the oil in a large skillet set over medium heat. Add the garlic and cook, stirring often, until aromatic, about 10 seconds. Add the shrimp and cook, stirring continuously, until pink and firm, about 3 minutes. Stir in the tomatoes and salt; cook for 1 minute, then remove the skillet from the heat.

3. Bring the broth to a simmer in a medium saucepan set over medium heat.

4. Warm the remaining 2 tablespoons oil in a large sauté pan set over medium heat. Add the onion and cook, stirring often, until translucent, about 3 minutes. Add the rice, spreading it evenly in the pan, and cook until lightly browned, about 2 minutes.

5. Drain the artichokes and add them to the rice. Cook for 1 minute, stirring continuously, then add the wine, stirring often, until the wine has been absorbed, about 3 minutes.

6. Pour in the hot broth and bring to a boil. Cover, reduce the heat, and simmer until the liquid has been mostly absorbed and the rice is tender, 18 to 20 minutes.

7. Remove the pan from the heat. Add the shrimp mixture, stirring gently to combine. Drizzle with oil and serve immediately.

POTATO GNOCCHI IN MEAT SAUCE WITH ROLLED BEEF GNOCCHI AL RAGÙ CON BRACIOLE

 6 servings

ADELINA ORAZZO ✳ When I was living in Casola, a farmer in a nearby town raised such highly prized potatoes that I'd have to place my order in July, for pickup after the harvest. I'd buy a *quintale*—just over 200 pounds—to last through the fall and winter. I've never tasted potatoes like those again, but Yukon Gold aren't bad as a substitute.

FOR THE GNOCCHI
1 pound **Yukon Gold potatoes**, peeled
1 cup **all-purpose flour**, plus more for
  rolling and dusting

FOR THE BRACIOLE
18 ounces **beef top round**, trimmed
  and cut into 6 (3-ounce) pieces
2 ounces **lard**, diced
1½ ounces **Pecorino Romano**, finely
  grated (about ⅓ cup)

2 tablespoons minced fresh **flat-leaf
  parsley**
2 teaspoons minced **garlic**
½ teaspoon **salt**
2 tablespoons **olive oil**

FOR THE MEAT SAUCE
2 tablespoons **olive oil**
½ cup chopped **onion**
1 pound **beef bottom round**, trimmed
  and cut into ¼-inch dice

4 cups canned crushed **tomatoes**
8 fresh **basil** leaves, finely chopped
½ teaspoon **salt**
½ teaspoon freshly ground **black pepper**

Fresh **basil** leaves, for garnish
Shaved **Parmigiano-Reggiano**, for
  garnish

1. To make the gnocchi, boil the potatoes in a large pot of water until tender, then pass them through a potato ricer into a large bowl. Gradually stir the flour into the potatoes, starting with ½ cup and then adding more little by little, until you have a soft dough that holds together without cracking. Add more flour if the dough seems sticky. Form the dough into a ball and set aside for 10 minutes.

2. Lightly flour a large baking sheet. Divide the dough into four even pieces and roll each into a log about ½ inch in diameter. Cut each log crosswise into ¾-inch pieces and arrange them in a single layer on the baking sheet. Cover with a kitchen towel and set aside.

3. To make the braciole, lay a large piece of plastic wrap on a clean work surface, set one piece of beef top round on the plastic wrap, and cover with a second piece of plastic wrap. Pound the meat to a ¼-inch thickness with the smooth side of a meat mallet or the bottom of a heavy saucepan, working with gentle but firm strokes so as not to tear the meat. Peel off the plastic wrap, set the meat aside, and repeat with the remaining meat pieces, changing the plastic wrap as necessary.

4. Lay the pounded meat pieces on a clean work surface. Divide the lard, Pecorino Romano, parsley, garlic, and salt evenly among them. Roll each piece tightly and secure closed with butcher's twine in at least two places.

5. Heat the oil in a large skillet set over medium heat. Add the beef rolls. Lightly brown on all sides, turning often, about 4 minutes. Transfer to a plate and set aside.

6. To make the meat sauce, heat the oil in the same skillet, then add the onion. Cook, stirring often, until softened, about 4 minutes. Add the beef bottom round and brown it well, stirring occasionally, about 5 minutes.

7. Add the tomatoes, basil, salt, and pepper. Raise the heat to high and bring the sauce to a boil. Slip the beef rolls into the sauce, reduce the heat, cover, and simmer, stirring occasionally, until both types of beef are tender, about 1 hour. Uncover the skillet and simmer the sauce until it's thick, about 5 minutes more. Cover and keep warm at the back of the stovetop.

8. Bring a large pot of water to a boil. Add the gnocchi and cook until they float, about 2 minutes. Drain well.

9. Transfer the beef rolls from the sauce to a cutting board. Snip off the twine and slice the rolls into ½-inch-thick pieces. Pour the gnocchi into the meat sauce; stir very gently, just to coat. Divide this mixture among six serving bowls; lay the sliced beef rolls in the bowls. Garnish with basil and Parmigiano-Reggiano.

POTATO GNOCCHI WITH PORCINI AND BROCCOLINI

GNOCCHI CON FUNGHI PORCINI E BROCCOLINI

 6 servings

NINA PICARIELLO ✳ Porcini mushrooms and broccolini are a hearty meatless accompaniment for gnocchi, brightened by a little orange zest.

3 tablespoons **olive oil**
1 tablespoon minced **garlic**
8 ounces fresh **porcini mushrooms**, finely chopped
1 pound **broccolini**, chopped
½ teaspoon **salt**

1 recipe **gnocchi** (page 91, steps 1 and 2), each dumpling rolled against the back of a fork's tines to make little grooves, or 1½ pounds fresh store-bought
Finely grated **orange zest**, for garnish

1. Bring a large pot of water to a boil.

2. Meanwhile, warm the oil and garlic in a large skillet set over medium heat. Cook until fragrant, stirring often, about 1 minute. Add the porcini; cook, stirring often, until they begin to release their liquid, about 2 minutes.

3. Add the broccolini and salt. Cook, tossing often, until the broccolini is tender, about 10 minutes. Turn off the heat and set aside at the back of the stove to keep warm.

4. Working in batches, add the gnocchi to the boiling water. Cook until they float, about 2 minutes. Use a slotted spoon to transfer the gnocchi to a serving dish. Top with the porcini and broccolini mixture. Garnish with orange zest and serve warm.

RICOTTA GNOCCHI IN TOMATO SAUCE

GNOCCHI DI RICOTTA AL SUGO DI POMODORO

 8 servings

TERESA SCALICI ✳ This is a different take on gnocchi, made with ricotta and flour instead of potatoes. Spinach and a basil pesto, classic additions, heighten the color and flavor. My sister and I used to make these with our nonna on Saturday night so they'd be ready for the family's Sunday dinner. To make them ahead, complete the recipe through step 2, cover the baking sheet, and refrigerate for up to 12 hours before cooking and serving.

FOR THE RICOTTA GNOCCHI
2 cups whole-milk **ricotta**
2 large **eggs**, at room temperature
3½ tablespoons frozen chopped **spinach**, thawed and squeezed dry

2½ tablespoons prepared **basil pesto**
¼ teaspoon freshly ground **black pepper**
4 to 6 cups **all-purpose flour**, plus more as needed

FOR THE SUGO DI POMODORO
3 tablespoons **olive oil**
½ cup chopped **onion**
1 tablespoon minced **garlic**
2 (28-ounce) cans whole **tomatoes**, drained

½ teaspoon **salt**
¼ teaspoon freshly ground **black pepper**

Freshly grated **Parmigiano-Reggiano**, for garnish

1. To make the ricotta gnocchi, combine the ricotta, eggs, spinach, pesto, and pepper in a medium bowl; stir well until evenly blended. Add 4 cups flour and stir until a soft dough forms, adding more flour as needed to keep the dough from being wet. Add just enough flour to make a soft, slightly sticky dough that holds its shape when you roll it into balls.

2. Lightly flour a clean work surface and a dry large baking sheet. Divide the dough into six even pieces; roll each into a long rope about 2 inches thick. Cut the ropes crosswise into 1-inch pieces and place the gnocchi on the baking sheet. Cover with a clean kitchen towel and set aside.

3. To make the sugo, set a deep skillet over medium-low heat for a couple of minutes. Swirl in the oil and add the onion. Cook, stirring often, until golden, about 15 minutes. Add the garlic and cook for 1 minute more.

4. Break each tomato open over the sink, scrape out the seeds, and crush it into the skillet. Stir in the salt and pepper, reduce the heat to low, and cook, stirring occasionally, until the tomatoes have broken down into a sauce, about 30 minutes.

5. Remove the skillet from the heat. Use an immersion blender to puree the sauce directly in the skillet until smooth, or carefully pour the sauce into a food processor and process until smooth.

6. Bring a large pot of water to a boil. Drop in the gnocchi. As soon as they rise to the surface, use a slotted spoon to transfer them to a serving dish. Top with the sugo and garnish with Parmigiano-Reggiano.

RICE BALLS NEAPOLITAN STYLE

ARANCINI ALLA NAPOLETANA

 6 servings

CARMELINA PICA ✳ These classic rice balls won me a job at my brother-in-law's Italian market because the customers who tried them kept saying, "These remind me of my nonna." They're crunchy on the outside and soft on the inside.

2 cups **arborio rice**
6 large **eggs**, at room temperature
2 ounces **Parmigiano-Reggiano**, finely grated (about ½ cup)
¼ cup packed fresh **flat-leaf parsley**, chopped

½ teaspoon **salt**
½ teaspoon freshly ground **black pepper**
2½ cups fresh **breadcrumbs**
8 ounces **mozzarella**, cut into 24 cubes
Canola or **vegetable oil**, for frying

1. Bring 4 cups water to a boil in a medium saucepan. Stir in the rice, cover, reduce the heat, and simmer until the rice is tender and the water has been absorbed, about 20 minutes.

2. Whisk 4 eggs, the Parmigiano-Reggiano, parsley, salt, and pepper in a large bowl until well blended. With a wooden spoon, slowly stir in the cooked rice until uniform. Set aside to cool to room temperature, about 1½ hours.

3. To make the rice balls, whisk the remaining 2 eggs in a medium bowl until smooth. Spread the breadcrumbs on a large plate. Clean your hands but do not dry them. Scoop up ¼ cup of the rice mixture and flatten it in your palms. Set a mozzarella cube in the center, then enclose the cheese in the rice and form the rice into a ball, sealing it well. Dip the ball in the beaten eggs, then roll it in the breadcrumbs, shaking off any excess. Set it aside and continue filling and forming rice balls until all the rice has been used, wetting your hands frequently so the rice doesn't stick. You'll end up with about 24 rice balls.

4. Line a large baking sheet with paper towels. Pour the oil into a large pot or Dutch oven to a depth of 3 inches. Clip a deep-frying thermometer to the inside of the pot and heat the oil over medium heat until it registers 325°F. Add 6 to 8 rice balls to the oil, without crowding, and fry, turning occasionally with a slotted spoon, until golden, about 4 minutes. Transfer the balls to the baking sheet and continue frying more rice balls, adjusting the heat to keep the oil's temperature constant. Serve hot.

VI

PASTA

JODY SCARAVELLA *What would Italian cuisine be without pasta? At its most basic, it's the* piatti poveri, *or poor people's food, that every culture has—filling, unpretentious, and honest. At its most lavish, it's an art form, with beautiful shapes designed to complement any topping and to delight the eye. But where the nonnas really get creative is with the sauces—from classic tomato-basil to any kind of meat or fish, or intriguing combinations like pumpkin, sausage, and chestnuts.*

Rosaria Vigorito

My first cooking experience was at my nonna's house, making peanut butter cookies out of a box. Yes, a box—my mother's parents emigrated from the Abruzzo region of central Italy to Youngstown, Ohio, to work in the steel mills. I can only imagine how curious Filomena Comichista, my nonna, must have been about American convenience foods.

My nonno, cousin, nonna, and aunt in Naples, 1950

We spent summers with her in Ohio, and I spotted the box in her kitchen. "I want to cook with you, Nonna," I said. "Please, can we make those cookies?"

"No," she told me. "But why don't you make them yourself?"

I was only six or seven, but I managed to grasp the directions. My nonna supervised but didn't help at all. That made me feel so proud, so empowered. When the cookies were done, they were delicious, but my sense of accomplishment was even sweeter. I felt like a master chef!

My younger siblings still remember those cookies, and I joke that they were the first crush in my lifelong romance with cooking. I'm the oldest of five, with a brother in Pennsylvania and sisters scattered around New York State. Every weekend, when they come to the city, they inevitably gather at my house—the place that has all the food.

But the cookies I associate most strongly with my nonna are *pizzelle,* a classic Abruzzi treat. They're made with lots of eggs (half a dozen), flour (about three and a half cups), lots of sugar (a cup and a half), and lots of butter (a full cup); flavored with anise oil or extract; and cooked over the gas stove in a special press, like a waffle iron with a slightly embossed snowflake design. My mother recently gave me one of my nonna's old pizzelle irons, and every time I use it, my nonna is with me. I feel her comforting presence, her gentleness.

My nonna was an expert baker. Every Saturday, she'd get up at four in the morning to bake bread for the coming week. Her pizzas were amazing, too, with perfect dough and an Old World topping of onions caramelized for hours in butter. The version I make today is quicker, with onions, tuna, and Gaeta olives, borrowed from a traditional Christmas Eve dish of my husband's family, who came from Bari, south of Abruzzo.

For pizza, my nonna swore by *doppio zero,* or "00," flour. In Italy, flours are categorized from the roughest grind, "1," to the finest, "000." The fineness of the grind affects the behavior of gluten; a finer grind yields a less elastic dough. Finely ground flour like "00" is not great for bread and pastries, but for pizzas and pasta, where you want just a bit of stretch, it gives great texture. It's one reason why Americans find that pasta and pizza taste different in Italy (another is Italian eggs, which have richer, orangier yolks).

Nowadays you can find anything online, including "00" flour. Still, I don't go out of my way to buy it, even for pizza. In America, my nonna got by on top-quality unbleached flour, with no additives, so that's become my staple.

But for pasta, I prefer to use semolina flour, which is made from hard durum wheat. You have to sift it with regular all-purpose flour, half-and-half, to make a pliable dough. I don't add salt or water; eggs are my only liquid. Sometimes, for extra zing, along with the eggs, I add Romano cheese and black pepper or minced parsley.

The classic Abruzzo way to cut pasta is with the *chitarra,* which is the Italian word for "guitar." It's a device resembling a musical instrument—an open, shallow box about a foot wide and two feet long, with closely spaced wires stretched tightly over its length. I roll my dough into a sheet about as thick as two stacked dimes and lay the sheet on the wires. When I make a firm pass over the sheet with a rolling pin, the wires slice the dough into strands, which drop into the box.

The strands of pasta have a squarish shape and a thinner width than can be easily cut by hand. Like hand-cut pasta, they have roughish edges, which capture sauces. Of course, a pasta machine can cut noodles just as efficiently but I affirm my heritage by using the chitarra, an ancient tool.

I cherished those summers in Ohio with my nonna, but it was very far from South Philly, where I grew up. There, we lived with my father's side of the family, who were Neapolitan. My mother had adapted to my father's taste—fattier, saltier, spicier—which was also more the standard in our largely southern Italian neighborhood. So, while I prized my nonna's pasta, pizzas, and bread—as well as her stories and patient teaching—I thought a lot of her food was bland. Now I know better, but I'd beg my mother back then, "Please, don't let her cook!"

How my family came together in America is one of those crazy immigrant stories. There was a lot of back-and-forth across the ocean in those days. In the early twentieth century, my father's father came to the States and struck it rich, actually wealthy enough to buy a hotel. Then something shady happened. This was around the time of Prohibition, so who knows if it was related to something like gangsters or liquor. Whatever it was, he lost all his money and fled back to Italy with his family.

My father's family was back in Italy at the time that Nonno Angelo, my mother's father, went to Ohio to seek work, and soon brought over the family, including Marianna, my mother. She was almost nineteen—practically an old maid in those days—and wanted to marry. She felt that she needed an Italian husband, who would understand her way of life. Her coworker, who happened to be my father's cousin, set up my parents as transatlantic pen pals. Letters and photos—that was their whole courtship. Finally, my mother popped the question, saying that, if her family approved, she would marry him.

Since her family was in America, my dad had to get the blessing of my mom's uncles in Abruzzo. Being exotic by Italian standards—

My nonno

blond and blue-eyed, with high, chiseled cheekbones—he was bound to make a good impression. But to clinch the deal, he brought along his brother Gabriele, who not only had similar movie-star looks but—major bonus!—was a priest. My great-uncles were convinced, but in approving the marriage, warned my mother, "You're going to have a lot of children with this man."

My mother bought a wedding dress and went to Italy. She and my dad met for the first time just a few days before they married. Strange as this may sound to us, such marriages weren't unusual at the time, which wasn't really all that long ago—the 1950s.

The newlyweds settled in Philadelphia, where my father's oldest sister, Zia Bina, lived. Her daughter Giovanna (Jenny), who is my godmother, practically raised me. But by the time my four siblings came along, we'd moved to Brooklyn, where my father got a better job and another of his sisters lived. Zia Adelaide's influence on our lives would be tremendous; for one thing, she taught my mother more about Neapolitan cooking, making *struffoli* a cornerstone of our holiday tradition. Loving and caring, she made us feel at home.

Still, my parents struggled with the language—so much so that, before I started school, my father insisted that my mother, who'd lived here longer, speak to me only in English. He thought that would give me an advantage. The funny thing was, she had such a strong accent that I picked it up. My classmates would laugh. "Oh, you're a guinea," they'd say, "You talk-a like this."

But New York is so diverse that I didn't stick out that much. I love the mix of cultures here, and it's made me value my own even more.

For as long as I could remember, I dreamed of getting married, having a family, and becoming the best cook in the world. Two of those longings I achieved. Like my mother, I married young. I had my first child at eighteen, and three more by my early twenties. I didn't want to be chasing after a teenager when I was forty or fifty. By that age, my mother and nonna had grandkids, and so do I—two so far. My grandson, Anthony, and my little granddaughter, Marianne, are my heart, the loves of my life.

As for becoming a cook, I joke that an Italian will make a feast out of anything, even a potato and an egg. In fact, one of my mother's signature school-day lunches was an omelet cooked in olive oil with a little onion, cheese, and cooked potatoes folded in. Or she'd make a salad of oranges with olive oil—always something interesting. At six o'clock, when my dad got home from work, we'd all race in to dinner, which was a serious multicourse meal, every single night. For Italian women of my mother's era, life was all about food, the main source of pleasure in a hardscrabble life. Their men would come home miserable and exhausted from tough jobs and find joy in their families, at the dinner table.

Even today, if you drop in and admit that you're hungry, my mother will whip up some homemade pasta. She'll say, "Just give me five minutes." Her fettuccine is as light as air, like silk in your mouth, and her ravioli, my favorite, is heavenly. It's simple—just ricotta, pecorino, parsley, and a couple of eggs, enveloped in handmade dough—but perfect.

PASTA WATER

⤙ ADELINA ORAZZO ⤚

I use bay leaves, especially fresh ones, in everything. My nonna used to say, "They not only add taste but they're very healthy, too. They keep your stomach in good condition." One of my special touches is adding a small bay leaf to the water I boil for pasta, to deepen the flavor and give it a lovely aroma.

SUMMER SAUCE

CHRISTINA NARISI CARROZZA

Every summer, my family has a couple of blowout canning days. My brother, Giuseppe, and his wife, Maria, live in New Jersey, with farms nearby, so we all descend on their house. From the farmers we buy bushels and bushels of vegetables—one year, nearly nine hundred pounds of tomatoes alone—to preserve for the winter. Giuseppe sets up little two-burner stoves in his yard, with massive pots. We fill those pots with halved tomatoes, and my mother, always the first one up, gets them boiling by 4:30 or 5:00 A.M. By the time the rest of us awaken, that first batch has boiled down and is ready to pass through the food mill. We use an electric one now because that step is so much work.

After the mill whirs out the seeds and skin, we return the pulp to the pots, add salt and basil, and let it reduce, while we sterilize dozens of jars. We jar the sauce, top it with olive oil, and stow the jars in the garage wrapped in blankets, for slow, even cooling. A jar shocked by a change in temperature will explode.

Meanwhile, in the kitchen, a second crew has been peeling, chopping, and sautéing eggplant and preparing other vegetables for eggplant salad or caponata. Once jarred, the caponata heads to the garage while another batch of tomatoes stews in the big pot—and so it goes, all day long, until we physically and mentally collapse.

One year, exhausted, I asked my mother, "Is it necessary to make everything at once? Why does this effort have to be so intense? It's so extreme!"

"Because we work, we live so far apart," she said, "You can never get everyone together for more than a day or two. And the beauty lies in doing it together."

She was right, of course.

Through my mother I've come to appreciate—and proudly represent—the Abruzzese cooking that I found bland (or too subtle) as a kid. Maybe your palate has to grow up, like everything else. A lot of what makes cooking "regional" is the herbs and spices. For example, saffron is a major flavoring in my mother's hometown. It's expensive here, so we didn't use it that often, but I sometimes add a few strands to the broth for my *crespelle*, to jazz it up.

104 ✳ NONNA'S HOUSE

Sage, which I love, is also important in Abruzzo. I add it to everything, from soup to pasta sauce. I grow it in a planter on my windowsill, along with rosemary, which is crucial for chicken and lamb. Fennel and nutmeg add lively notes. Basil, parsley, and bay leaves are staples, of course. When I assemble my herbs and spices, I feel like a kitchen witch.

But making "regional" dishes is just a foundation. Borrowing and adapting are what make cooking fun. Take struffoli, the Neapolitan treat, which is basically fried dough dipped in honey, that my mother borrowed from Zia Adelaide and made part of our Christmas tradition. Every year, my whole family—my brother and sisters, their children, and the grandkids—gathers to crank out pounds of them.

My mother prepares the dough, and we each get a lump. Some of us roll it out and cut it into ribbons, using tools that look like miniature fluted pizza wheels, then form each ribbon into a rosette. Others make the classic shape by rolling out pencil-size logs of dough, then cutting them into segments. Batches of each are fried in hot oil and then set on the big table, covered with absorbent paper, to drain and cool. Meanwhile, a huge pot of honey is heating on the stove. It's so heavy and thick that no spoon can get through it; you have to stir it with a rolling pin. When the honey is warm and thinned, we use it to glaze the struffoli, arranging them in clusters. The classic ones, but not the rosettes, get decorated with colored sprinkles. The whole process is so much fun.

Obviously, not even borrowing helped me achieve my dream of becoming the best cook in the world. When my kids were old enough—I was about twenty-seven—I went back to school to become a special ed teacher. Now I counsel children one-on-one by day, and by night, I cook at the Enoteca.

That's an education in itself. The nonnas come from different generations and different places, so they have many useful tricks. Simple ones, like a Sicilian nonna throwing a handful of breadcrumbs into a pan of spaghetti with marinara. "What are you doing?" I asked, as she mixed it in. "It thickens the sauce. This is our way," she said.

There's always something new to learn in the kitchen. Always some new way to feed people well, which I think sustains them spiritually as well as physically. They feel the love, the energy you put into making a dish delicious. It's all about creativity.

I love the inspirations.

FRESH PASTA

HOW TO ROLL, CUT, AND COOK PASTA

It seems as if every nonna has her own special pasta dough. The two doughs here are particular favorites among our *nonnas*: one with flour for a soft, tender noodle, and one with a little semolina flour for a little more chew.

   With either recipe, you can use the following instructions for rolling, cutting, and cooking the pasta.

1. To roll out the dough by hand, divide the dough into four even pieces. Keep the pieces wrapped or covered until you're ready to roll them. On a lightly floured work surface, form one of the pieces of dough into a flattened rectangle. Use a rolling pin to roll one piece of dough, working from the center out to each edge, keeping the rectangular shape. With each roll, you are relaxing the glutens, so let the dough rest a moment in between. Flip the dough over once or twice, lightly flouring the surface beneath it to prevent sticking. Roll to the desired thickness, usually about ⅛ inch. Cover the rolled sheet with plastic wrap or a second clean kitchen towel, set aside, and roll the remaining pieces of dough.

   Alternatively, to roll out the dough with a pasta machine, divide the dough into four even pieces. Keep the pieces

wrapped or covered until you're ready to roll them. On a lightly floured work surface, form one of the pieces of dough into a flattened rectangle. Pass the rectangle through the rollers of the machine, starting with the widest setting. Fold the dough in half and again pass through at the widest setting. Repeat five times to let the glutens relax. Lightly dust with flour as needed to prevent sticking. Then decrease the space between the rollers, one notch at time, and pass the dough through until it reaches the desired thickness, usually about ⅛ inch.

2. To cut the dough by hand, place one rolled-out sheet on a lightly floured work surface. Lightly dust it with flour and fold it in half lengthwise. Dust the top surface with flour and again fold the dough in half lengthwise, to form a rectangle four layers thick. With a sharp knife, slice through the lay-

ers crosswise to create strands of the desired width—for example, about ⅓ inch for fettuccine, slightly wider for tagliatelle, about ¾ inch for pappardelle. Pick up the cut strands and shake them to straighten, dust lightly with flour, and repeat the process with the remaining sheets.

Alternatively, to cut the dough with a pasta machine, use the attachment with teeth spaced at the desired width and pass the dough through it. Pick up the cut strands and shake them to straighten, dust lightly with flour, and repeat the process with the remaining sheets.

3. To cook fresh pasta, bring a large pot of lightly salted water to a boil, add the pasta, and boil until al dente—soft but retaining a slight bite—for 1 to 5 minutes, depending on the width of the noodles. Drain well, then add to your prepared sauce.

BASIC EGG PASTA DOUGH PASTA ALL'UOVO

4 to 6 servings

CHRISTINA NARISI CARROZZA

- 3 cups **all-purpose flour**, plus more for dusting
- 4 large **eggs**, at room temperature, well beaten
- 2 tablespoons **olive oil**
- ⅛ teaspoon **salt**

Stir all the ingredients in a large bowl with 2 tablespoons water until a dough forms. Turn out the dough onto a lightly floured surface and knead by hand for 8 to 10 minutes, until soft and smooth—or stir the dough in the bowl of a stand mixer and use the mixer's hook attachment to knead the dough on medium speed for 4 to 5 minutes. Form the dough into a ball. Cover with plastic wrap or a clean kitchen towel and set aside at room temperature for 30 minutes, then roll out and cut the pasta as described on pages 106–107.

SEMOLINA PASTA DOUGH PASTA DI SEMOLA

4 to 6 servings

ROSARIA VIGORITO

2 cups **semolina flour**
2 cups **all-purpose flour**, plus more
  for dusting

6 large **eggs**, at room temperature,
  well beaten
1 tablespoon **olive oil**

Sift the flours together into a mound on a clean work surface. Make a deep well in the center of the mound. Pour the eggs into the well and add the oil. Begin whisking the eggs gently with a fork, gradually incorporating the flour from the sides of the well. As the dough thickens, begin mixing with your hands. Knead until smooth and soft, 8 to 10 minutes. If the dough is sticky, dust it and the work surface with more flour. When the dough is supple, wrap it tightly in plastic wrap and set aside at room temperature for 30 minutes, then roll out and cut the pasta as described on pages 106–107.

SIMPLE TOMATO SAUCES FOR PASTA

Each of these everyday, simple but delicious recipes will yield enough sauce for a pound of pasta—either six first-course servings or four main-course servings.

FRESH BASIL SAUCE

CHRISTINA NARISI CARROZZA ✳ About 3 cups

2 tablespoons unsalted **butter**
5 tablespoons **olive oil**
1 tablespoon minced **garlic**
4 cups canned crushed **San Marzano tomatoes**
½ teaspoon **salt**
¼ teaspoon freshly ground **black pepper**
¼ teaspoon **red pepper flakes**
¾ cup packed fresh **basil**, minced

Heat the butter and oil together in a medium saucepan, then add the garlic and cook, stirring often, until golden brown, about 2 minutes. Add the tomatoes, salt, black pepper, and red pepper flakes and simmer until thickened, about 20 minutes. Before serving, stir in the basil.

CHERRY TOMATO PASTA SAUCE WITH PORCINI

ROSARIA VIGORITO ✳ About 3 cups

6 dried **porcini mushrooms**
½ cup **olive oil**
2 tablespoons minced **garlic**
1 quart **cherry tomatoes**, halved
¼ cup packed fresh **flat-leaf parsley**, chopped
½ teaspoon **salt**
¼ teaspoon freshly ground **black pepper**
¼ teaspoon **red pepper flakes**, or to taste

In a small, heatproof bowl, cover the porcini with boiling water and soak until softened, about 30 minutes. Reserving the soaking liquid, remove the porcini with a slotted spoon, squeeze them dry, and dice them. Heat the oil in a medium saucepan, add the garlic and cook, stirring often, until lightly browned, about 1 minute. Add the tomatoes, parsley, salt, black pepper, and red pepper flakes; then cook, stirring often, until the tomatoes begin to break down, about 15 minutes. Then add the porcini, along with some of the soaking liquid, strained to remove any grit, and cook until the sauce is thickened, about 15 minutes.

SAUCE OF TOMATO "FILLETS," NEAPOLITAN STYLE

CARMELINA PICA ✳ About 2½ cups

2 cups drained canned whole **tomatoes**
3 tablespoons **olive oil**
½ cup chopped **onion**
1 teaspoon minced **garlic**
½ teaspoon **salt**
⅛ teaspoon **red pepper flakes**
1 cup dry **white wine**
Minced fresh **flat-leaf parsley** or **basil**, for garnish

Seed the tomatoes and then slice them lengthwise into ¼-inch-thick strips. Heat the oil in a medium saucepan, add the onion, and cook, stirring often, until softened, about 3 minutes. Add the garlic and cook for about half a minute before stirring in the tomato strips, salt, and red pepper flakes. Bring to a simmer, add the wine, and cook until the tomatoes have started to break down, about 5 minutes. Garnish with parsley or basil.

MY NONNA'S TOMATO AND EGGPLANT SAUCE

TERESA SCALICI ✳ About 3 cups

4 tablespoons **olive oil**
2 teaspoons minced **garlic**
1 medium Italian **eggplant**, peeled and cut into ½-inch cubes (about 2½ cups)
8 ounces **cherry tomatoes**, halved
½ teaspoon **salt**
½ teaspoon freshly ground **black pepper**
Finely grated **Parmigiano-Reggiano**, for garnish

Heat the oil in a large skillet, add the garlic, and cook, stirring often, until golden, about 2 minutes. Add the eggplant and cook, stirring occasionally, until lightly browned, 8 to 10 minutes. Add the tomatoes, salt, and pepper; cook, stirring occasionally, until the tomatoes break down and the eggplant is tender, about 30 minutes. Sprinkle with Parmigiano-Reggiano before serving.

SIMPLE NUT SAUCES FOR PASTA

Each of these tasty recipes yields enough sauce for a pound of pasta—that is, six first-course servings or four main-course servings.

WALNUT SAUCE FOR FETTUCCINE

CHRISTINA NARISI CARROZZA ✳ About 1½ cups

½ cup **walnut** pieces, toasted and cooled

½ cup **mascarpone**

2 ounces **Parmigiano-Reggiano**, finely grated (about ½ cup)

¼ cup packed fresh **flat-leaf parsley**, minced

¼ cup extra-virgin **olive oil**, plus more as needed to thin the sauce.

Put all the ingredients in the food processor and pulse to a creamy paste-like consistency.

NEAPOLITAN-STYLE PESTO FOR BUCATINI

CARMELINA PICA ✳ About 2½ cups

5 cups packed fresh **basil**

3 medium **plum tomatoes**, seeded and chopped

¼ cup sliced **almonds**

1 **garlic** clove

¼ cup extra-virgin **olive oil**

¼ teaspoon **salt**

½ cup sliced pitted **black olives**

Shaved **provolone**, for garnish

Put the basil, tomatoes, almonds, and garlic in the food processor and chop coarsely. Scrape down the inside of the canister, add the oil and salt, and pulse to a paste-like consistency. Before serving, stir in the olives and sprinkle with provolone.

AMALFI-STYLE NUT SAUCE FOR SPAGHETTI

NINA PICARIELLO ✳ About 2 cups

⅓ cup **walnut** pieces, toasted and cooled
⅓ cup raw **almonds**, toasted and cooled
6 tablespoons **olive oil**
8 canned **anchovy fillets**, minced
1 teaspoon minced **garlic**
2 jarred roasted whole **red peppers** or **pimientos**, cut into ½-inch-thick strips
Toasted chopped **walnuts** and/or **almonds**, for garnish if desired

While the nuts are cooling, heat the oil, add the anchovies and garlic, and cook, stirring often, until the garlic softens and starts to brown. Add the red peppers and stir until heated through, about 1 minute. Combine in the food processor with the nuts and pulse until chunky.

PAPPARDELLE WITH PORCINI IN CREAM SAUCE

PAPPARDELLE AI FUNGHI PORCINI E PANNA

 6 servings as a pasta course or 4 as a main course

ROSA TURANO ✳ My brother-in-law is crazy about this sauce. I prefer to make it with the Italian dried porcini because they're bigger, without crumbly bits. Look for dried porcini in large unbroken pieces in the packet.

1 ounce dried **porcini mushrooms**

2 tablespoons unsalted **butter**

1 tablespoon **olive oil**

4 medium **shallots**, minced (about 1 cup)

1 tablespoon fresh **thyme**, chopped

¾ cup **heavy cream**

1 pound dried **pappardelle**, cooked and drained

3 ounces **Parmigiano-Reggiano**, finely grated (about ¾ cup)

1. Bring 2 cups water to a boil in a small saucepan. Set the porcini in a small bowl and pour in the boiling water. Soak until soft, about 20 minutes. Set a colander over a bowl and drain the porcini, reserving the liquid. Strain the liquid through a cheesecloth or a coffee filter to get rid of any grit. Chop the porcini into small pieces. Set both aside.

2. Melt the butter in the oil in a deep skillet set over medium heat. Add the shallots and cook, stirring often, until golden, about 4 minutes.

3. Add the porcini and thyme; cook, stirring occasionally, until fragrant, about 1 minute. Pour in the soaking liquid and raise the heat to high. Bring the mixture to a boil and cook, stirring often, until the liquid has been reduced to a thick glaze, about 7 minutes.

4. Pour in the heavy cream, stir well, and return the sauce to a simmer. Add the pappardelle and toss with tongs to coat. Pour into a serving bowl or individual bowls and top with the Parmigiano-Reggiano.

PENNE WITH RADICCHIO, WALNUTS, AND GORGONZOLA

PENNE AL RADICCHIO, NOCI E GORGONZOLA

6 servings as a pasta course or 4 as a main course

CHRISTINA NARISI CARROZZA ✳ Radicchio can be bitter when it's raw. Cooking brings out a little of its sweetness, which makes it a better match for Gorgonzola. My mother used to make this recipe in the winter because it was such a colorful addition to the holiday table.

2 tablespoons unsalted **butter**

5 tablespoons **olive oil**

1 medium **onion**, chopped (about 1 cup)

2 ounces **pancetta**, coarsely chopped

3 small heads **radicchio**, cored, thinly sliced, and shredded

1½ pounds dried **penne**, cooked and drained

¼ cup packed fresh **flat-leaf parsley**, chopped

2 ounces **Parmigiano-Reggiano**, finely grated (about ½ cup)

¼ cup chopped **walnuts**, toasted

½ teaspoon **salt**

½ teaspoon freshly ground **black pepper**

4 ounces **Gorgonzola**, crumbled (about 1 cup)

1. Melt the butter in the oil in a large saucepan set over medium heat. Add the onion and pancetta; cook, stirring often, until the onion is translucent, about 4 minutes. Add the radicchio and cook, stirring often, until wilted and tender, about 3 minutes.

2. Stir in the penne, parsley, Parmigiano-Reggiano, walnuts, salt, and pepper. Toss well until the penne is heated through and well coated. Divide among serving bowls and sprinkle with Gorgonzola.

PASTA WITH BROCCOLI IN A POT

PASTA CON BROCCOLI IN TEGAME

 6 servings as a pasta course or 4 as a main course

MARGHERITA AMATO ✳ My mother's little store in Casteldaccia sold vegetables raised on her land, among other local and staple products. Broccoli and cauliflower were customer favorites. We call the dish *in tegame* because we make it in a pot instead of a skillet and sometimes bring the pot right to the table to serve the pasta.

2 tablespoons **olive oil**
1 medium **onion**, chopped (about 1 cup)
⅓ cup **raisins**
⅓ cup **pine nuts**
8 canned **anchovy fillets**, chopped
3 cups small **broccoli** florets
1 cup **vegetable broth**
½ teaspoon **saffron**

¼ teaspoon **salt**
¼ teaspoon freshly ground **black pepper**
1 pound dried **penne**, cooked and drained
½ cup fresh **breadcrumbs**, toasted in the oven until golden, then cooled
1 teaspoon **sugar**
Extra-virgin **olive oil**, for garnish

1. Warm the oil in a large saucepan or pot set over medium heat. Add the onion and cook, stirring occasionally, until golden, about 10 minutes. Add the raisins, pine nuts, and anchovies; cook, stirring continuously, until the pine nuts brown a bit, about 2 minutes.

2. Add the broccoli and cook, stirring occasionally, until warmed through, about 2 minutes. Pour in the broth; stir in the saffron, salt, and pepper. Raise the heat to medium-high and bring the sauce to a boil. Cook, stirring occasionally, until the broccoli is al dente, about 5 minutes.

3. Add the penne. Toss and stir until it absorbs any liquid remaining in the pot.

4. Remove from the heat and sprinkle with the breadcrumbs and sugar. Drizzle with extra-virgin olive oil before serving.

SPAGHETTI WITH POTATOES AND CABBAGE

SPAGHETTI CON PATATE E VERZE

 6 servings as a pasta course or 4 as a main course

CHRISTINA NARISI CARROZZA ✳ This is a classic northern Italian recipe. I've always thought that potatoes and cabbage are to my region what eggplant and broccoli rabe are to Sicily.

4 medium russet **potatoes** (about 1½ pounds), peeled and cut into ½-inch cubes

1 small **savoy cabbage**, cored, thinly sliced, and shredded

2 tablespoons unsalted **butter**

2 teaspoons minced **garlic**

¾ cup **heavy cream**

8 ounces **Fontinella**, shredded (about 2 cups)

4 ounces **Parmigiano-Reggiano**, finely grated (about 1 cup)

¼ teaspoon **salt**

¼ teaspoon freshly ground **black pepper**

1 pound dried **spaghetti**, cooked and drained

1. Bring a large pot of water to a boil. Add the potatoes and cook for 10 minutes. Add the cabbage and cook until both vegetables are tender, about 5 minutes more. Drain well.

2. Melt the butter in a deep skillet set over medium heat. Add the garlic and cook until fragrant, about 10 seconds. Do not brown the garlic. Add the potatoes and cabbage; toss well to heat through.

3. Stir in the heavy cream, Fontinella, Parmigiano-Reggiano, salt, and pepper. Cook until bubbling, stirring often, about 2 minutes. Add the spaghetti and toss with tongs until well coated. Serve immediately.

SPAGHETTI WITH SEA URCHINS

SPAGHETTI AI RICCI DI MARI

 4 servings

ELVIRA PANTALEO ✳ Sea urchins make a delicate and beautiful pasta sauce. This traditional dish is one of my specialties. Sea urchins can be found at many good fish markets and Italian or Asian markets, as well as online.

12 **sea urchins** (4 to 6 ounces each)
1 tablespoon **salt**
1 pound dried **spaghetti**
¾ cup extra-virgin **olive oil**
½ cup minced fresh **flat-leaf parsley**,
  plus more for garnish

1 tablespoon minced **garlic**
1 cup dry **white wine**
Red pepper flakes, for garnish

1. To open the sea urchins, insert the tips of a pair of kitchen shears into the small opening on the flat (or bottom) side of the urchin. Cut a small slit off this opening, then snip around the shell until you can crack open the urchin in two pieces. Use a small spoon to remove the orange pulp, discarding all the black liquid and everything else inside. Continue with the remaining urchins; set the pulp aside.

2. Bring a large pot of water to a boil. Add the salt and then the spaghetti. Reduce the heat and cook the spaghetti until al dente, about 7 minutes. Reserve 1 cup of the cooking water, then drain the spaghetti.

3. Warm the oil in a deep skillet set over medium heat until rippling, about 3 minutes. Add the parsley and garlic; cook, stirring occasionally, until fragrant, about 2 minutes.

4. Add the cooking water and the wine. Bring to a simmer and cook until only about ½ cup of the liquid remains in the skillet, about 10 minutes.

5. Remove the skillet from the heat and stir in half the sea urchin pulp. Add the cooked spaghetti and set the skillet back over medium heat. Toss well but gently to heat through, about 1 minute. Add the remaining pulp, toss very gently, and immediately divide among serving plates, garnishing with parsley and red pepper flakes.

ZITI WITH FRESH SARDINES, FENNEL, AND BREADCRUMBS

ZITI CON SARDE, FINOCCHIO E PANGRATTATO

6 servings as a pasta course or 4 as a main course

MARGHERITA AMATO ✳ This is one of the dishes we traditionally serve on St. Joseph's Day. In my town, an essential addition was our local wild fennel, but you can use regular fennel stalks and fronds.

10 **fennel stalks** and **fronds** (from 3 or 4 bulbs; about 1½ cups), coarsely chopped
4 tablespoons **olive oil**
½ cup fresh **breadcrumbs**
1 medium **onion**, chopped (about 1 cup)
⅓ cup **raisins**
⅓ cup **pine nuts**

6 canned **anchovy fillets**, chopped
1 (28-ounce) can crushed **tomatoes**
2 tablespoons **sugar**
¼ teaspoon **salt**
¼ teaspoon freshly ground **black pepper**
1 pound small fresh **sardines**, cleaned
1 pound dried **ziti**, cooked and drained

1. Bring a large pot of water to a boil. Add the fennel stalks and fronds; cook for 2 minutes, then drain.

2. Warm 2 tablespoons of the oil in a deep skillet set over medium-high heat. Add the breadcrumbs and toss until toasty brown, about 3 minutes. Scrape them into a bowl and wipe out the skillet with paper towels.

3. Set the skillet back over medium-high heat, put in the remaining 2 tablespoons oil, then the onion. Cook, stirring often, until golden, about 10 minutes. Reduce the heat to medium and add the raisins, pine nuts, and anchovies. Cook, stirring frequently, until the pine nuts begin to brown, about 3 minutes.

4. Stir in the fennel stalks and fronds; cook until fragrant, about 1 minute. Add the tomatoes, sugar, salt, and pepper. Reduce the heat to low and cook, stirring occasionally, until the tomatoes begin to break down, about 20 minutes.

5. Add the sardines and cook, stirring gently, until the sardines are cooked through and the sauce has a thick, velvety consistency, about 10 minutes. Gently stir in the ziti until coated. Divide among serving plates and top with the toasted breadcrumbs.

FRESH FETTUCCINE WITH TUNA, EGGPLANT, AND MINT

FETTUCCINE CASARECCE AL TONNO CON MELANZANE E MENTA

6 servings as a pasta course or 4 as a main course

ELVIRA PANTALEO ✳ Mint and red pepper flakes add lively notes to this dish. Use only fresh pasta—it will be soft and delicious with the tuna. Make sure the eggplant is tender after you first cook it since it won't really cook again in this simple pasta dish.

2 medium Italian **eggplants** (about 1½ pounds total), peeled and cut into ¼-inch dice

1 tablespoon plus ¼ teaspoon **salt**

4 tablespoons **olive oil**

2 pounds **cherry tomatoes**, halved

¼ cup packed fresh **flat-leaf parsley**, minced

2 teaspoons minced **garlic**

1 cup dry **white wine**

1 pound **tuna fillets**, cut into ½-inch cubes

1½ pounds homemade **fettuccine** (one and a half times the **Basic Egg Pasta Dough** recipe on page 108), or fresh store-bought

½ cup loosely packed fresh **mint**, chopped

¼ teaspoon **salt**

Red pepper flakes, for garnish (optional)

1. Toss the eggplant and the 1 tablespoon salt in a large bowl and set aside for 30 minutes. Rinse the eggplant in a colander, drain well, and dry on paper towels laid across your work surface.

2. Warm 3 tablespoons of the oil in a large nonstick skillet set over medium heat until rippling. Add the eggplant and cook, stirring often, until golden brown at the edges and tender, 7 to 10 minutes. Use tongs to transfer the eggplant to a large bowl.

3. Add the remaining 1 tablespoon oil to the skillet, and then add the tomatoes, parsley, and garlic. Bring to a brisk simmer and cook, stirring often, until the tomatoes begin to soften, about 2 minutes.

4. Pour in the wine and return to a simmer. Cook, stirring often, until the tomatoes break down and the sauce has reduced to about two-thirds of its original volume.

5. Add the tuna, stir gently, and cook for 5 minutes. Stir in the eggplant, fettucine, mint, and the ¼ teapoon salt until well combined and cook until heated through, about 2 minutes. Serve immediately, garnishing with red pepper flakes, if desired.

PAPPARDELLE WITH SALMON, ZUCCHINI, AND WALNUTS

PAPPARDELLE AL SALMONE CON ZUCCHINI E NOCI

6 servings as a pasta course or 4 as a main course

CHRISTINA NARISI CARROZZA ✳ Pappardelle and salmon look beautiful together. This dish is tempting even for those who don't like fish. I like to garnish the dish with grated Parmigiano-Reggiano as well as with chopped walnuts, but you might prefer a simpler flavor.

1 tablespoon unsalted **butter**

3 tablespoons **olive oil**

3 medium **zucchini**, cubed (about 3 cups)

2 teaspoons minced **garlic**

¼ cup medium-dry **white wine**

8 ounces **salmon fillet**, skin removed and flesh cubed

2 tablespoons chopped fresh **basil** leaves, plus more leaves for garnish

½ teaspoon **salt**

½ teaspoon freshly ground **black pepper**

1 pound dried **pappardelle**, cooked and drained

Toasted chopped **walnuts**, for garnish

1. Melt the butter in the oil in a deep skillet set over medium heat. Add the zucchini and cook, stirring often, until tender, about 6 minutes.

2. Add the garlic and cook for less than a minute, just until fragrant. Stir in the wine and scrape up any browned bits from the bottom of the skillet.

3. Add the salmon, basil, salt, and pepper. Cook, stirring very gently to keep the fish together, until the salmon is cooked through, about 3 minutes. Stir in the pappardelle and toss very gently with tongs to coat. Divide among serving plates and top with basil leaves and walnuts.

LAGANE and CHICKPEAS with SHRIMP

LAGANE E CECI CON GAMBERI

8 servings as a pasta course or 6 as a main course

NINA PICARIELLO ✳ *Lagane* are large pieces of pasta with irregular shapes. They're hard to find in North America, but you can break up lasagna noodles to get a good result. These flat pieces of pasta complement the textures of chickpeas and shrimp in my pasta dish.

2 tablespoons **olive oil**

1 tablespoon minced **garlic**

1 pound medium **shrimp** (about 30 per pound), peeled and deveined

1 cup canned **chickpeas**, drained and rinsed

¼ teaspoon **salt**

¼ teaspoon freshly ground **black pepper**

1½ pounds dried **lasagna noodles**, broken into irregular 1½-inch pieces, cooked and drained

Minced fresh **flat-leaf parsley**, for garnish

1. Warm the oil in a deep skillet set over medium heat. Add the garlic and cook until sizzling and fragrant, about 2 minutes.

2. Add the shrimp, chickpeas, salt, and pepper. Cook, stirring often, until the shrimp are pink and firm, about 4 minutes. Add the pasta and toss well to coat; cook for 1 minute to heat through. Divide among serving dishes and sprinkle with parsley.

CALAMARATA with MUSSELS and EGGPLANT

CALAMARATA CON COZZE E MELANZANE

 *6 servings as a pasta course or 4 as a main course*

NINA PICARIELLO ✳ Calamarata pasta, which is shaped like rings of calamari, has a heft that works well with ingredients like mussels and eggplant.

3 pounds **mussels**, scrubbed and debearded
¼ cup **canola oil**, plus more as needed
2 medium Italian **eggplants** (about 1½ pounds), peeled and cut into ½-inch cubes
1 cup **all-purpose flour**
1 teaspoon **salt**
½ teaspoon freshly ground **black pepper**

2 tablespoons **olive oil**
1 tablespoon minced **garlic**
8 ounces **cherry tomatoes**, halved
8 fresh **basil** leaves, minced
2 tablespoons packed fresh **flat-leaf parsley**, chopped
1 pound dried **calamarata**, cooked and drained

1. Bring 1 inch of water to a boil in a large saucepan. Add the mussels, cover, and steam until they open, about 6 minutes. Drain the mussels in a colander and refresh under cool water; discard any mussels that have not opened. Pull the meat out of the shells, saving 6 or 8 mussels in their shells for garnish. Place the mussel meat in a small bowl and discard the shells.

2. Warm the canola oil in a deep skillet set over medium heat. Toss the eggplant, flour, salt, and pepper in a large bowl. Shake off the excess flour, then add enough eggplant to the skillet to form a single layer without crowding. Brown the eggplant on all sides, turning often, about 6 minutes. Use tongs to transfer the eggplant to the bowl with the mussels, and continue frying eggplant, adding more canola oil to the skillet if needed.

3. Drain any remaining canola oil, then heat the olive oil in the skillet. Add the garlic and cook until sizzling, about 1 minute. Add the tomatoes, basil, and parsley; cook, stirring often, until the tomatoes begin to break down, about 3 minutes.

4. Return the eggplant and mussels to the skillet. Cook for 1 minute, then add the calamarata and toss well to coat and heat through, about 1 minute. Divide among individual plates.

SCIALATIELLI WITH CLAMS, MUSSELS, AND CRAB SCIALATIELLI CON VONGOLE, COZZE E GRANCHI

 4 servings

NINA PICARIELLO ※ Scialatielli is a style of pasta associated with the Neapolitan Amalfi Coast. It's long, like fettuccine, but thicker.

1 tablespoon **olive oil**
2 small **zucchini** or yellow **crookneck squash**, thinly sliced (about 2 cups)
1 small **onion**, diced (about ½ cup)
8 ounces **grape** or **cherry tomatoes**
2 tablespoons minced fresh **basil**
½ teaspoon **salt**
½ teaspoon freshly ground **black pepper**
4 tablespoons (½ stick) unsalted **butter**, cut into chunks

1 pound small **clams**, such as Manila, scrubbed
1 pound **mussels**, scrubbed and debearded
1 pound dried **scialatielli**, cooked and drained
½ pound lump **crabmeat**, picked over for shell and cartilage
Minced fresh **flat-leaf parsley**, for garnish

1. Warm the oil in a deep skillet set over medium heat. Add the zucchini, onion, tomatoes, basil, salt, and pepper. Cook, stirring often, until the zucchini is tender, 8 to 10 minutes.

2. Add the butter and stir until it melts. Add the clams and mussels. Cover, reduce the heat to low, and cook until the clams and mussels open, about 8 minutes. Discard any that do not open.

3. Add the scialatielli and crabmeat; toss gently to heat through, about 1 minute. Divide among serving bowls and garnish with parsley.

LINGUINE WITH OCTOPUS SAUCE

LINGUINE AL SUGO DI POLPETTI

6 servings as a pasta course or 4 as a main course

NINA PICARIELLO ✳ Cleaned baby octopus is available in most Italian markets and fish markets, and even in the freezer section of many big supermarkets.

3 pounds **baby octopus**, cleaned
3 tablespoons **olive oil**
1 tablespoon minced **garlic**
¼ cup dry **white wine**
2 pounds **cherry tomatoes**, halved
½ teaspoon **salt**

½ teaspoon freshly ground **black pepper**, plus more for serving
¼ teaspoon **red pepper flakes**
1 pound dried **linguine**, cooked and drained
Torn fresh **flat-leaf parsley**, for garnish

1. Bring a large saucepan of water to a boil. Add the octopus, cover, and boil until tender, about 20 minutes. Drain.

2. Warm the oil in a deep skillet set over medium heat. Add the garlic and cook until browned, about 2 minutes. Add the wine and bring to a simmer. Cook, stirring occasionally, until the liquid has reduced to a thick glaze, 4 to 5 minutes.

3. Add the tomatoes, salt, black pepper, and red pepper flakes. Stir well and cook for 2 minutes. Add the octopus and the linguine; toss gently to combine. Cook for 1 minute to heat through. Divide among serving bowls and garnish with black pepper and parsley.

LINGUINE WITH CUTTLEFISH AND ITS INK

LINGUINE AL NERO DI SEPPIA

4 servings

ELVIRA PANTALEO ✳ This Italian classic is one of my signature dishes. The ink from *seppia* (cuttlefish) blackens the pasta, making for a dramatic presentation. Cuttlefish can be found at Italian, Asian, and many good fish markets.

2 large **cuttlefish** with their ink sacs
3 tablespoons **olive oil**
2 medium **onions**, chopped (about 2 cups)
2½ cups dry **white wine**
⅓ cup **sugo di pomodoro** (page 95) or **plain marinara sauce**

½ teaspoon **salt**
½ teaspoon freshly ground **black pepper**, plus more for serving
1 pound dried **linguine**, cooked and drained
Torn fresh **flat-leaf parsley**, for garnish

1. Separate the ink sacs from the cuttlefish and set aside. Pull back the tentacles and remove the bones. Pinch off and discard the "beak." Turn the head inside out, remove the stomach and discard. (If you're squeamish, ask your fishmonger to do this step for you.) Rinse the heads and tentacles thoroughly, pat dry, and cut into small pieces.

2. Warm the oil in a deep skillet set over medium heat. Add the onions and cook, stirring often, until golden brown, about 10 minutes.

3. Add the wine and cuttlefish meat. Cook, stirring occasionally, until the wine has reduced to a thick glaze, about 15 minutes.

4. Stir in the sugo, salt, pepper, and the reserved ink sacs as well as 1 cup warm water. Cover, reduce the heat to low, and cook, stirring occasionally, for 30 minutes, adding more water if the skillet looks dry.

5. Add the linguine and toss well to coat. Transfer to a serving platter or to individual plates. Garnish with pepper and parsley before serving.

TAGLIATELLE with PUMPKIN and CHESTNUTS

TAGLIATELLE CON ZUCCA E CASTAGNE

4 servings

ADELINA ORAZZO ✳ In Naples, a traditional topping for pasta is chestnuts with butternut squash or pumpkin. When I was young, I used to go the mountainside to gather chestnuts and porcini mushrooms. This recipe includes my own special semolina pasta, just enough to go with my version of this classic sauce.

FOR THE PASTA

2⅓ cups **all-purpose flour**

⅔ cup **semolina flour**, plus more for dusting

¼ teaspoon **salt**

3 large **eggs**, at room temperature

FOR THE SAUCE

1 (1- to 1¼-pound) **butternut squash** or **pumpkin**, peeled, seeded, and cut into 1-inch cubes

4 tablespoons **olive oil**

1 teaspoon chopped fresh **rosemary**

¼ teaspoon ground **cinnamon**

¼ teaspoon **salt**

¼ teaspoon freshly ground **black pepper**

2 **bay leaves**

1 small **onion**, chopped (about ½ cup)

1 pound sweet Italian **pork sausage**, casings removed

1 cup dry **white wine**

8 ounces jarred roasted **chestnuts**, sliced

Finely grated **Pecorino Romano**, for garnish

1. To make the pasta, whisk both flours and the salt in a large bowl until well combined. Make a well in the center of the mixture and add the eggs. Beat the eggs with a fork until smooth, then collapse more and more of the flour into the center, beating all the while, until the mixture forms a soft dough. Form into a ball, cover with a clean kitchen towel, and set aside at room temperature for 30 minutes.

2. Knead the dough and roll it out following the instructions on pages 106–107. Cut into ½-inch-wide strips for tagliatelle. Dust a large baking sheet with semolina flour, gather the strips into loose wads, set them on the baking sheet, and cover with a clean kitchen towel.

3. Position the rack in the center of the oven and preheat the oven to 400°F.

4. To make the sauce, mix the squash, 2 tablespoons of the oil, the rosemary, cinnamon, salt, and pepper on a large rimmed baking sheet. Tuck the bay leaves under the squash.

Bake until the squash is tender and begins to caramelize at the edges, 25 to 30 minutes. Transfer to a wire rack; discard the bay leaves.

5. Bring a large pot of water to a boil. Meanwhile, warm the remaining 2 tablespoons oil in a deep skillet set over medium heat. Add the onion and cook, stirring occasionally, until softened, about 4 minutes. Crumble in the sausage; cook, breaking it up with the back of a wooden spoon and stirring occasionally, until browned, 8 to 10 minutes.

6. Pour in the wine and bring to a simmer. Cook, stirring occasionally, until the liquid in the skillet has reduced to about ¼ cup. Transfer the roasted squash to the skillet, add the chestnuts, toss gently, and remove from the heat.

7. Add the tagliatelle to the boiling water. Cook until al dente, 2 to 3 minutes. Drain. Add the tagliatelle to the skillet with the sauce and toss gently. Divide among serving bowls and garnish with Pecorino Romano.

SPAGHETTI WITH BROCCOLI RABE, SAUSAGE, AND CREAM SPAGHETTI CON RAPINI, SALSICCIA E PANNA

 6 servings as a pasta course or 4 as a main course

TERESA SCALICI ✳ I add cream to this dish to give it a rich flavor but also, more important, to tenderize the sausage, which can stiffen when sautéed in oil. The cream also offsets any bitterness in the broccoli rabe.

4 cups chopped **broccoli rabe** (about
  ½ pound)
3 tablespoons **olive oil**
1 large **onion**, diced (about 1½ cups)
1½ pounds hot **Italian sausage**, cut into
  1-inch pieces

1 cup **heavy cream**
1 pound dried **spaghetti**
8 ounces **mozzarella**, cubed

1. Bring a large pot of water to a boil. Add the broccoli rabe and blanch for 3 minutes, then remove the pot from the heat. Reserving the blanching water, use a slotted spoon to transfer the broccoli rabe to a large bowl.

2. Warm the oil in a deep skillet set over medium heat. Add the onion; cook, stirring often, until softened, about 4 minutes. Add the sausage and cook, stirring often, until browned and cooked through, about 10 minutes.

3. Stir in the broccoli rabe and heavy cream. Bring to a simmer, then cover and remove from the heat.

4. Bring the water in the pot back to a boil. Add the spaghetti and cook until al dente, about 7 minutes. Drain.

5. Serve in a large pasta bowl, building it like this: the hot spaghetti first, then the mozzarella sprinkled over the spaghetti, then the cream sauce poured on top. Serve it once the mozzarella has melted, about 2 minutes.

VII

PASTE IMBOTTITE e PIZZA

JODY SCARAVELLA *As a child with a Sicilian grandmother, I tried to love all those complicated layered baked dishes—lasagna, pasta al forno—that she lovingly prepared on Sundays. It was years before I realized that the point of those dishes wasn't just to, say, honor the Lord's Day, but to clean out the fridge. Today I smile at that memory and recognize, of course, that pasta* imbottita—imbottita *means "stuffed" or "padded"—like lasagna, cannelloni, manicotti, and the rest are artful compositions worthy of being the anchor of any Italian feast.*

Adelina Orazzo

One of my favorite childhood memories is of waking in the middle of the night to a delicious smell, then sneaking into the kitchen to find my father eating soup. Not just any soup, but our ancient and traditional *minestra*

My wedding day, 1974

maritata, served on holidays because it was too much work to be an everyday pleasure. Minestra maritata was my father's specialty, and he'd make so much that we'd share it with the neighbors. The name refers to the "marriage" of its ingredients— lots of meats and vegetables joined together.

A day ahead, my father would start the stock, a brew of guinea hen and stew beef, and separately boil preserved pork trimmings—including the snout, ears, and tail—to remove the salt. All the vegetables he added came from his garden, and the main ones—chicory, escarole, and *verʒa* (savoy cabbage)—were also simmered separately to reduce their bitterness. On the holiday itself, he'd add the cooked pork and vegetables to the chicken, beef, and broth in his gigantic pot, and heat everything together. Our holiday main course was often cannelloni or lasagna, but it's that soup—and its amazing aroma—that I always associate with celebration.

My father wasn't a cook by trade, but a carpenter. He worked on the Isle of Capri, across the bay from Casola, our little town on the outskirts of Naples. Since his commute was long, he came home only once a week. My mother boosted the family finances with a seasonal job in a tomato-canning factory. During the months she worked, when I was very young, my father's parents looked after my two sisters, two brothers, and me, the oldest.

I got my first exposure to cooking from my nonna. She didn't even have a common wood-burning stove but, rather, a brick firebox with a heavy metal cooktop. You'd build a fire in the brick section, and to cook, you'd use a spike to lift one of the disks cut into the top. Each disk covered a hole into which you could lower a pot, so its bottom would be close to the flames. Though I was too small to try such heavy lifting myself, I was fascinated.

My grandfather made wine, but because of his asthma, he needed help crushing the grapes. Crates of grapes were dumped into a huge vat. He told me, "Get in there and start stomping them. It will give you strong legs." So I did, along with a bunch of my girlfriends. The whole time, we were giggling and fooling around. But I remember once, for some reason, being stuck doing it alone, walking around that vat, squashing the grapes under my feet, all night long.

By the time I was eight, my grandparents were too infirm to handle us, so I inherited the job of watching my brothers and sisters, along with keeping house.

By then, my parents' hard work had enabled them to buy a small apartment. It had two sections, divided by a courtyard. On one side was the room where my parents slept, and across the courtyard were the kitchen and the kids' bedroom, with sleeper couches, that doubled as the living room. When we first moved in, the floor was packed earth. Until we could afford a real floor, we'd mix up a dark brown finishing compound and brush it over the surface. Then, with a string, we'd press a grid pattern into the earth to give it the look of tile. We had electricity and cooking gas, but no running water. For washing and cooking, we fetched water from the neighborhood spigot in a large kettle made of lightweight copper.

To wash clothes— which became my responsibility—we'd reverse the journey, hauling dirty laundry to the *lavanderia*, or communal washing station. The water there was icy cold, even in the hottest weather. By the time I finished scrubbing the clothes, my hands were frozen into claws, too stiff to open.

Then, at around age ten, I saw my first washing machine. What a wonder! I wanted one desperately. In my piggybank, I'd saved the coins that relatives and neighbors gave me for things like reciting Christmas poems. So I begged my mother, "Let's break open the bank. Maybe I've saved enough to buy a washer." Of course, I didn't quite grasp that, to have a washing machine, we'd need to get running water.

But my mother, being good with money, found a way to fulfill my dream, and from the town hall, she got the necessary permits to run a water line into our home. I still remember that it cost 20,000 lira in the late 1960s—equal to roughly $20 today—to bring my family into the modern world.

I was eleven when we finally got the washer. Since there was no local sewer system, we had a makeshift plumbing setup, with the wastewater spewing out the door, onto the ground. But I was thrilled and did laundry till my back ached. The beloved washing machine was installed right next to my bed. The following year, we marched even further into the twentieth century by buying a refrigerator on an installment plan.

Though we had to scrimp and save for such luxuries, we were never short of food. Our vegetables—eggplants, peppers, and more—were fresh from my father's and grandparents' gardens. We'd preserve them for the winter in terra-cotta crocks. On the hillside, we could gather porcini mushrooms and chestnuts. We raised chickens, for eggs and meat, as well as rabbits, on our roof. Maybe once a week, we'd buy other kinds of meat from a local farmer, alone or with another family chipping in.

There was also a lot of sharing in our tight community. For example, if one family bought a pig, they'd eat and preserve a lot of it and give away the rest. Naturally, you'd want to repay a favor like that—which is what led me to invent a special dish.

It was a kind of *polpetta*, or meatball. Every Sunday, my mother would wake up early to collect and soak our dried bread, mix it with whatever meat and other scraps she had, and fry meatballs to add to her sauce when we got home from church. She'd hide the meatballs from us kids, but we'd usually manage to sniff them out and steal a few. Naturally, meatballs were one of the dishes that I loved to make.

To thank the neighbors who'd given us some pork, I was preparing meatballs the usual way when I noticed a big bowl of eggs on the kitchen table. I decided to boil some eggs, wrap them in meat, brown the outside, and finish the meatballs in the oven. I arranged them on a bed

My uncle Matteo selling watermelon, 1950

Women fetching water at the town fountain in Casola, 1948

of greens on a beautiful platter. When I brought over the dish, the size of the meatballs, which were gigantic, stunned the neighbors. "Just try one," I said. "You're in for a surprise." They loved them, of course, but couldn't resist asking, "Where do you get these ideas?"

I didn't really have an answer except that, to feed my siblings, all along I'd been experimenting in the kitchen. When my mother learned that her eight-year-old was cooking for the kids, she was thrilled. "Go ahead and make whatever you want," she said. "I know that you'll do a good job." So, by trial and error, I developed a sense of combinations, learning which flavors went together. I was completely free to be creative, with no adult around making rules.

When I was eleven, my mother honored my cooking by suggesting, "Why don't you make an engagement dinner for your aunt?" People in the family had heard about my experiments. I decided to make cannelloni with a filling of beef, ricotta, and mozzarella, with chicken cacciatore as the second plate. "What will be the antipasto?" my mother asked. I saw that my father had brought home a big basket of figs. I got the idea to wrap the figs in prosciutto, for a nice balance of sweetness and saltiness. The dinner, for forty-five guests, was a huge success. No one could believe that the cook behind the meal wasn't even in her teens.

By the time of that dinner, my school years were winding down. I still had childcare duties, so I did piecework at home, sewing woolen linings for winter gloves. I was approaching marriageable age, and I needed to earn money for a wedding gown.

Naples, my city, is known for its love songs. Perhaps the most famous is "A Marechiare," recorded by singers around the world, including Luciano Pavarotti. It describes the moon rising in the sky over a darkening beach, as village girls wait at their windows for their beloved fishermen to come home from the sea. It begins, "When the moon comes out in Marechiare, even the fish are making love . . ."

So I had a dreamy impression of courtship. Perhaps a suitor would serenade me with a song like "A Marechiare." That didn't happen when I got engaged, which happened when I was thirteen years old. I was eighteen when I married Michele.

Shortly after our marriage, we moved to Milan, where Michele had gotten a job as a waiter in a hotel. My first child, Carolina, was born there. But when one of Michele's sisters died, he wanted to be close to his family. We resettled in Casola, and Michele became the chief quality control officer for the area's cheese-making authority, famous for its provolone.

Casola was a comfortable place to raise children, surrounded by family and friends. During July and August, mothers and children spent nearly every day at the beach. On weekends, the husbands would join us. I'd wake up at five in the morning to make picnic food and would even pack a little camp stove. Often a big group of us would go together, staking out a spot for our umbrellas and chairs and letting the kids run free. We'd connect with our beach friends, people who we never saw anywhere else. It was like a daily party in our seasonal community.

There was a woman who always sat on a rock, soaking her legs in the water. Her husband would be out netting anchovies, which the two of them would pack into crocks and sell, right there on the beach. All of us would buy containers of anchovies, fresh from the sea, to bring home. Sometimes the husband would take his canoe out farther, to where the water was cleaner, and return with just-plucked mussels in a mesh bag. Michele, who also fished for mussels, would cook them, and they'd vanish in an instant. I was lucky ever to get a single one.

We'd stay till nearly sunset. Then at home, after the kids were showered and asleep, I'd wash all the towels and hang them to dry for the next day's trip to the beach. Those were very happy times.

By the late 1980s, my brother-in-law had immigrated to America. We went to visit and realized that we might find better job opportunities here. So we took a chance and immigrated with our five children—Carolina, Domenico, Raffaele, Francesco, and Antonio—who ranged in age from fifteen to three. Our youngest, Anna, was born in the States. But within a few years, Michele grew gravely ill. He survived, but the marriage didn't. The new millennium found me raising my younger children alone, in Brooklyn.

It was my niece who spotted the newspaper ad seeking nonnas to cook at the Enoteca. I was thrilled when Jody told me the same thing my mother had, fifty years ago: "Go ahead and make whatever you want." It's interesting to see that, while most of the nonnas cook the same basic dishes, the way they turn out is wildly different.

Everything we make comes out of our traditions and our life experience. Think how much broader our experience is than that of our mothers, stuck in their villages, without the global communication that we have today. But, of course, that exposure just gives you new ideas; more fuel. How you use them depends on your imagination.

BASIC PIZZA DOUGH PIZZA, IMPASTO BASE

about 1½ pounds

ADELINA ORAZZO ✳ I make my pizza dough with Italian *doppio zero* or "00" flour, a very soft, high-protein flour that yields the most tender pizza crust. It's available online, but all-purpose flour is fine. If you don't want to make your own pizza dough, you can find fresh dough in the refrigerator case of many large supermarkets or Italian markets. Most pizzerias are also willing to sell you a lump. Don't use canned dough or frozen rolled-out pizza crusts.

¾ cup plus 1 tablespoon warm **water** (105° to 115°F), plus more as needed
1 (¼-ounce) package active dry **yeast** (2¼ teaspoons)
1 teaspoon **sugar**

½ teaspoon **salt**
2 teaspoons **olive oil**, plus more for the bowl
3⅓ cups **"00" flour** or **all-purpose flour**, plus more as needed

1. Pour the warm water into a large bowl; stir in the yeast, sugar, and salt until dissolved. Set aside until foamy, about 5 minutes.

2. Stir in the oil, then the flour to create a soft dough, adding more warm water in 1 tablespoon increments to ensure that the dough holds its shape without cracking. Form the dough into a ball and turn it out onto a lightly floured work surface. Knead for 10 minutes, twisting and pulling the dough with one hand against the work surface while digging the heel of the other hand into the lump, folding the dough onto itself, readjusting, and doing it again and again, until the dough is smooth and soft. Add more flour in small amounts if the dough is sticky. Gather the dough into a ball.

3. Lightly oil a large bowl and set the dough into it. Turn the dough over, cover the bowl with a clean kitchen towel, and set aside in a warm, draft-free place until the dough doubles in bulk, about 1½ hours. The dough is now ready for use in any of the recipes in this chapter.

STUFFED FRIED DOUGH CRESCENTS PANZEROTTI

6 servings

ROSARIA VIGORITO ✳ *Panzerotti* are like smaller fried calzones. It was my in-laws' tradition to make them for Christmas Eve as a group project, with my father-in-law rolling out the dough, my mother-in-law frying, and everyone else helping with fillings. But panzerotti are enjoyable any time of year, with any filling you want: peppers, onions, mushrooms, different cheeses, salami, or sausage—you name it. Just be sure not to overfill them.

8 ounces **mozzarella**, shredded (about 2 cups)
4 ounces **provolone**, shredded (about 1 cup)
4 ounces **fontina**, shredded (about 1 cup)
6 canned **anchovy fillets**, minced
1 tablespoon drained and rinsed **capers**, chopped

1 recipe **Basic Pizza Dough** (page 146), or 1½ pounds store-bought
¾ cup **sugo di pomodoro** (page 95) or **plain marinara sauce**
Vegetable oil, for frying

1. Stir the mozzarella, provolone, fontina, anchovies, and capers in a large bowl. Set aside.

2. Divide the dough into six equal pieces; roll each piece into an 8-inch circle. Place 2 tablespoons of sugo across half of each circle, leaving a ½-inch border. Top each with 2½ tablespoons of the cheese mixture. Fold closed to form a crescent and seal tightly, crimping the edges with the tines of a fork.

3. Set a layer of paper towels on a clean work surface and set a wire rack on top. Pour oil into a large pot or Dutch oven to a depth of 2 inches. Clip a deep-frying thermometer to the inside of the pot and heat the oil over medium heat until it registers 350°F.

4. Add half the crescents to the hot oil, without crowding, and fry until golden brown, about 4 minutes, gently turning once. Adjust the heat to keep the oil's temperature constant. Use a slotted spoon to transfer the crescents to the wire rack to drain, and fry the remaining crescents. Serve hot.

5. Alternatively, bake the crescents instead of frying them. Position the rack in the center of the oven and preheat the oven to 400°F. Lightly oil a large rimmed baking sheet; arrange the crescents on the baking sheet, spacing them at least 2 inches apart. Brush lightly with oil. Bake until golden brown, about 20 minutes. Cool on the baking sheet for 10 minutes before serving.

SICILIAN PIZZA WITH MOZZARELLA, SCALLIONS, AND ANCHOVIES SFINCIONE

4 to 6 servings

MARGHERITA AMATO ✳ We make different versions of *sfincione*: some fried, some baked, for different occasions. This is one that we traditionally serve on Christmas Eve.

⅓ cup **olive oil**, plus more for the pan
8 **scallions**, thinly sliced (about ⅔ cup)
6 canned **anchovy fillets**, finely chopped
1 (28-ounce) can **tomato puree**
1 tablespoon **sugar**
½ teaspoon **salt**
¼ teaspoon freshly ground **black pepper**

1 recipe **Basic Pizza Dough** (page 146), or 1½ pounds store-bought
6 ounces fresh **mozzarella**, shredded (about 1½ cups)
2 teaspoons minced fresh **oregano**
4 ounces **Parmigiano-Reggiano**, finely grated (about 1 cup; optional)

1. Warm the oil in a large skillet set over medium heat. Add the scallions and cook, stirring often, until golden brown, about 3 minutes. Add the anchovies and stir until they almost dissolve, about 3 minutes. Add the tomato puree, sugar, salt, and pepper. Bring the sauce to a brisk simmer, then reduce the heat to low and cook, stirring often, until thickened, about 20 minutes. Scrape the sauce into a bowl and let cool for 10 minutes.

2. Position the rack in the center of the oven and preheat the oven to 375°F. If making a circular pie, set a pizza stone in the oven to preheat as well.

3. For a circular pie, dust a pizza peel with flour. Press the dough on the peel, stretching it and dimpling it with your fingertips, to form a 12-inch circle, shaking the peel repeatedly to make sure the dough isn't sticking. To make a rectangular pie, lightly oil an 11 x 17-inch rimmed baking sheet. Press and dimple the dough into a slightly irregular 10 x 14-inch rectangle.

4. Spoon the tomato sauce onto the dough, leaving a ½-inch border around the pie. Sprinkle the mozzarella evenly over the sauce, leaving the border uncovered. Sprinkle with the oregano and Parmigiano-Reggiano, if using. For a circular pie, shake the peel to make sure the pie isn't sticking and slide it onto the preheated pizza stone. For a rectangular pie, set the baking sheet in the oven.

5. Bake until golden and bubbling, 15 to 20 minutes. Slip the peel under the circular pie and remove it from the oven—or set the rectangular pie in its baking sheet on a wire rack. Let cool for 10 minutes. Slice into wedges, squares, or rectangles and serve hot.

ONION AND TUNA PIZZA PIZZA CON CIPOLLE E TONNO

 ———————————————————— *4 to 6 servings* ⊢——⊣

ROSARIA VIGORITO ✳ This is a dish that my in-laws, from Bari, served on Christmas Eve, but it's so delicious that I've borrowed it as an anytime treat. Sometimes I make it with a traditional crust, but I actually prefer the phyllo option, which gives it a nice crunch.

3 tablespoons **olive oil**, plus more as needed
1 large **onion**, halved and cut into thin half-moons
1 (5-ounce) can Italian **tuna** packed in olive oil, drained

¼ cup pitted **black olives**, preferably Gaeta, chopped
¼ cup **golden raisins**
½ teaspoon freshly ground **black pepper**
8 ounces frozen **phyllo sheets**, thawed
Small fresh **basil** leaves, for garnish

1. Warm the oil in a large skillet set over low heat, then add the onion. Reduce the heat to very low and cook, stirring often, until the onion is deep brown, soft, and sweet, 35 to 40 minutes. Stir in the tuna, olives, raisins, and pepper. Remove from the heat.

2. Position the rack in the middle of the oven and preheat the oven to 350°F. Line an 11 x 17-inch rimmed baking sheet with parchment paper. Brush the paper lightly with oil.

3. Unwrap the phyllo sheets and place them under a sheet of plastic wrap and then a clean kitchen towel. Remove 1 phyllo sheet, re-cover the stack, and set the phyllo sheet in the center of the prepared parchment paper. Brush lightly with oil, then repeat, making a stack of 8 phyllo sheets. Make a ½-inch border around the phyllo by folding the edges of the sheets up and over themselves; press the border down so it stays in place.

4. Spoon the onion mixture evenly over the phyllo. Bake until the crust is golden and crisp, about 35 minutes. Let cool on the baking sheet on a wire rack for 10 minutes before garnishing with basil leaves and slicing the phyllo into squares or rectangles. Serve hot.

ESCAROLE AND OLIVE PIZZA

PIZZA CON SCAROLA E OLIVE

 4 to 6 servings

ADELINA ORAZZO ✳ Escarole has an earthiness and a slight bite that make this pizza especially appealing.

1 small head **escarole** (about 12 ounces), cored and leaves separated
2 tablespoons **olive oil**, plus more for the pan
¼ cup pitted **black olives**, halved
4 canned **anchovy fillets**, chopped

2 **garlic** cloves, slivered
¼ teaspoon **red pepper flakes**
¼ teaspoon **salt**
1 recipe **Basic Pizza Dough** (page 146), or 1½ pounds store-bought
2 teaspoons minced fresh **oregano**

1. Bring a large pot of water to a boil. Add the escarole and cook for 3 minutes, making sure the leaves are submerged. Drain in a colander. Use the back of a wooden spoon to press out the excess moisture. Transfer to a cutting board and let cool for 15 minutes. Chop the escarole into bite-size pieces.

2. Position the rack in the center of the oven and preheat the oven to 350°F. Lightly oil an 11 x 17-inch rimmed baking sheet.

3. Warm the oil in a large skillet set over medium heat. Add the olives, anchovies, garlic, red pepper flakes, and salt. Cook, stirring often, until sizzling, about 2 minutes. Add the escarole and toss well to combine. Remove from the heat to cool for 10 minutes.

4. Press the dough onto the baking sheet, stretching and dimpling it with your fingertips into a 10 x 14-inch oval. Spoon the escarole mixture over the dough, leaving a ½-inch border around the pie. Sprinkle with the oregano.

5. Bake until the crust is puffed and golden and the topping is lightly browned, about 30 minutes. Transfer to a wire rack to cool in the pan for 10 minutes, then slice into wedges, squares, or rectangles to serve.

RAVIOLI WITH RABBIT FILLING

RAVIOLI DI CONIGLIO

 8 servings as a pasta course or 6 as a main course

TERESA SCALICI ✳ The only challenge in making this dish is being sure to remove all the bones, which I do by carefully running the meat through my fingers. It's delicious even when made with leftover cooked rabbit. If you don't want to make your own pasta dough, you can buy 1½ pounds of fresh lasagna sheets as a stand-in.

FOR THE RABBIT FILLING
3 tablespoons **olive oil**
2 **rabbit hind legs** (about 1 pound)
½ cup minced **onion**
2 teaspoons minced **garlic**
1 (28-ounce) can crushed **tomatoes**
¼ teaspoon **salt**
¼ teaspoon freshly ground **black pepper**

1 ounce **Parmigiano-Reggiano**, finely grated (about ¼ cup), plus more for garnish
½ ounce **mozzarella**, shredded (about 2 tablespoons), plus more for garnish

FOR THE PASTA DOUGH
3 cups **"00" flour** or **all-purpose flour**, plus more as needed
¼ teaspoon plus 1 tablespoon **salt**

¾ cup warm **water**, or as needed
1 tablespoon **vegetable oil**

1. To make the rabbit filling, warm the olive oil in a large sauté pan set over medium heat. Add the rabbit and cook until browned on both sides, turning once, about 7 minutes. Transfer to a large bowl.

2. Add the onion to the pan and cook, stirring often, until golden, about 3 minutes. Add the garlic, cook for about 30 seconds, then stir in the tomatoes, salt, and pepper. Return the rabbit and any juices that have collected in the bowl to the pan. Bring to a brisk simmer, stirring up any browned bits on the bottom of the pan. Cover, reduce the heat, and cook until the rabbit is tender, about 40 minutes. Transfer the rabbit to a cutting board; let cool for 20 minutes. Let the pan cool slightly, then cover it and refrigerate.

3. Debone the rabbit and place the meat in a food processor fitted with a chopping blade. Pulse until finely chopped; transfer to a medium bowl. Stir in the Parmigiano-Reggiano, mozzarella, and 1 tablespoon of the tomato sauce from the pan. Cover and refrigerate.

4. To make the pasta dough, put the flour and ¼ teaspoon of the salt in a large bowl, make a well in the middle, and gradually stir in warm water until the ingredients come together to form a soft dough. If the dough will not form into a ball, add more water, a few teaspoons at a time; if the dough is sticky, add flour in tiny increments until soft. Gather the dough into a ball and knead on a lightly floured work surface until smooth and elastic, about 10 minutes. Seal in plastic wrap and set aside at room temperature for 30 minutes.

5. Cut the dough in half; cover the unused portion. Roll out the dough to a thickness of ⅛ inch with a rolling pin or with a pasta machine, using the techniques described on pages 106–107. If using a rolling pin, aim to make a 12 x 16-inch rectangle on a lightly floured work surface. Cover the rolled-out dough with a dry kitchen towel as you repeat the process with the second piece of dough.

6. Take the rabbit filling out of the refrigerator. Cut each pasta sheet into eight 2 x 12-inch strips. Cover all but two strips and set aside, then place six 1-teaspoon mounds of filling along one strip of dough, spacing them 2 inches apart. Place the other strip on top; press between and around each mound of filling to seal. Slice each small piece of ravioli apart with a paring knife or a pastry cutter. Set the cut ravioli on a large baking sheet in a single layer and cover with a clean kitchen towel. Repeat with the remaining fourteen pasta strips to create a total of 48 ravioli.

7. Set the pot with the tomato sauce over medium-low heat, cover, and bring to a simmer. Bring a large pot of water with the remaining 1 tablespoon salt and the vegetable oil to a boil.

8. Drop half the ravioli into the boiling water. As soon as they rise to the surface, scoop them out with a slotted spoon, drain well, and place in a serving dish. Repeat with the remaining ravioli. Pour the warmed tomato sauce over the ravioli and sprinkle with Parmigiano-Reggiano and mozzarella before serving.

CANNELLONI WITH MEAT-AND-RICOTTA STUFFING CANNELLONI NAPOLETANI

 4 to 6 servings

ADELINA ORAZZO ✳ Since I was eleven years old, cannelloni has been one of my specialties. I consider this a jewel in my personal collection of traditional recipes.

FOR THE TOMATO SAUCE
2 tablespoons **olive oil**
½ cup chopped **onion**
2 teaspoons minced **garlic**

1 (28-ounce) can crushed **tomatoes**
½ teaspoon **salt**
½ teaspoon freshly ground **black pepper**

FOR THE FILLING
2 tablespoons **olive oil**
1 pound lean **ground beef**
1 cup whole-milk **ricotta**
8 ounces **mozzarella**, shredded (about 2 cups)

1 large **egg**, lightly beaten
¼ cup finely minced **basil**
¼ teaspoon **salt**
¼ teaspoon freshly ground **black pepper**

FOR THE CASSEROLE
1 recipe **Adelina's pasta dough** (page 135), or 12 dried medium **cannelloni tubes**, cooked and drained

Finely grated **Parmigiano-Reggiano**, for garnish
Torn fresh **basil** leaves, for garnish

1. To make the tomato sauce, warm the oil in a large saucepan set over medium heat. Add the onion and cook, stirring often, until softened, about 3 minutes. Stir in the garlic; cook until fragrant, about 20 seconds. Stir in the tomatoes, salt, and pepper. Bring to a boil, then reduce the heat and simmer until reduced by half, about 15 minutes. Cover and set aside off the heat to keep warm.

2. To make the filling, warm the oil in a medium skillet set over medium heat, then crumble in the ground beef. Cook, breaking up the beef and stirring occasionally, until fully browned, about 7 minutes. Transfer to a large bowl and let cool for 15 minutes.

3. Stir the ricotta, mozzarella, egg, basil, salt, and pepper into the beef until well combined.

4. Position the rack in the center of the oven and preheat the oven to 350°F.

5. To make the casserole, spread ½ cup of the tomato sauce over the bottom of a 9 x 13-inch baking dish.

6. Cut the pasta dough into three equal pieces. Roll out the dough to a thickness of ⅛ inch with a rolling pin or with a pasta machine, using the techniques described on pages 106–107. If using a rolling pin, aim to roll out an 8 x 12-inch rectangle on a lightly floured work surface. Cut the dough into 4 x 6-inch sheets and cover with a dry kitchen towel as you repeat the process with the second and third pieces of dough.

7. Place ¼ cup of the beef filling along the 6-inch edge of one 4 x 6-inch piece. Roll it closed like a cigar, then place it seam side down over the tomato sauce in the baking dish. Continue filling and rolling the remainder of the pasta rectangles and setting them in the dish in a single layer. If using cooked dried tubes, fill each tube with ¼ cup of filling and set the tubes in the dish in a single layer.

8. Pour the remaining tomato sauce over the cannelloni. Bake until bubbling and lightly browned, about 20 minutes. Transfer to a wire rack and sprinkle with Parmigiano-Reggiano. Let cool for 5 minutes as the cheese melts, then garnish with basil.

SPINACH MANICOTTI MANICOTTI DI SPINACI

 4 to 6 servings

CARMELINA PICA ✳ My manicotti are similar to cannelloni in that both use individual sheets of dough to enclose the filling, but I cook mine like crepes before I roll them.

FOR THE FILLING
2 cups whole-milk **ricotta**
8 ounces **mozzarella**, shredded (about 2 cups)
¼ cup frozen chopped **spinach**, thawed and squeezed dry
1 large **egg**, at room temperature, lightly beaten

1 ounce **Pecorino Romano**, finely grated (about ¼ cup)
2 tablespoons minced fresh **flat-leaf parsley**
½ teaspoon freshly ground **black pepper**

FOR THE CREPES
2 large **eggs**, at room temperature
1 cup **all-purpose flour**

Cooking spray

FOR THE CASSEROLE
2½ cups **sugo di pomodoro** (page 95) or **plain marinara sauce**

2 ounces **Pecorino Romano**, finely grated (about ½ cup)

1. To make the filling, stir the ricotta, mozzarella, spinach, egg, Pecorino Romano, parsley, and pepper in a medium bowl until well combined.

2. To make the crepes, whisk the eggs and ⅔ cup water in a medium bowl until uniform. Whisk in the flour in a slow, steady stream until smooth, without any lumps.

3. Coat an 8-inch nonstick skillet with cooking spray and set over medium heat for a couple of minutes. Pour 2 tablespoons of the batter into the skillet and swirl to coat evenly. Cook for 1 minute, then peel up and flip the crepe with tongs. Cook for about 10 seconds, until just lightly browned. Transfer to a plate. Repeat with the remaining batter, making 12 crepes.

4. Position the rack in the center of the oven and preheat the oven to 325°F.

5. To make the casserole, spread 1 cup sugo over the bottom of a 9 x 13-inch baking dish. Spread ¼ cup of the cheese filling on each crepe, and roll closed. Set the crepe seam side down in the baking dish and continue filling more crepes, arranging them in a single layer in the dish. Cover with the remaining sugo, then sprinkle with the Pecorino Romano.

6. Cover with aluminum foil and bake for 30 minutes. Uncover and let cool on a wire rack for 10 minutes before serving hot.

CALABRIAN BAKED PASTA CASSEROLE

PASTA AL FORNO CALABRESE

 6 to 8 servings

FRANCESCA LEONE ✳ This traditional dish with pork meatballs was served at my wedding, but it's not only for formal celebrations. In the summertime, we used to get up early in the morning and make a big dish of it to bring to the mountains for a picnic.

FOR THE TOMATO SAUCE
2 tablespoons **olive oil**, plus more for the baking dish
1 medium **onion**, halved and cut into thin half-moons
4 ounces cured, aged **pork sausage**, casings removed and meat diced
1 (28-ounce) can **tomato puree**
¼ teaspoon **salt**
¼ teaspoon freshly ground **black pepper**

FOR THE MEATBALLS
¾ cup fresh **breadcrumbs**
4 ounces **ground pork**
1 ounce **Parmigiano-Reggiano**, finely grated (about ¼ cup)
2 tablespoons minced fresh **flat-leaf parsley**
1 large **egg yolk**
1 teaspoon minced **garlic**
¼ teaspoon **salt**
¼ teaspoon freshly ground **black pepper**

FOR THE CASSEROLE
1 pound dried **ziti**, cooked and drained
8 ounces **provolone**, grated (about 2 cups)
2 hard-boiled **eggs**, peeled and chopped
4 ounces **Pecorino Romano**, finely grated (about 1 cup)

1. To make the sauce, warm the oil in a large pot or Dutch oven set over medium heat. Add the onion and cook, stirring often, until soft and golden, about 10 minutes. Add the pork sausage, cook, stirring frequently, until it begins to release its fat, about 3 minutes.

2. Add the tomato puree, salt, and pepper and bring to a boil, stirring often to get the browned bits off the bottom of the pot. Cover, reduce the heat, and simmer.

3. To make the meatballs, mix the breadcrumbs, ground pork, Parmigiano-Reggiano, parsley, egg yolk, garlic, salt, and pepper in a medium bowl until well combined. Using wet hands, form 1 tablespoon of the mixture into a small ball and drop it into the pot of tomato sauce. Repeat with the remainder of the mixture, making about 16 meatballs.

4. Cover the pot and cook the meatballs in the sauce for 5 minutes. Stir gently and continue simmering until the sauce has thickened and the meatballs are cooked through, about 15 minutes.

5. Position the rack in the center of the oven and preheat the oven to 375°F. Lightly grease a 9 x 13-inch baking dish.

6. Gently stir the ziti into the sauce, then the provolone and the eggs. Pour the mixture into the baking dish and spread it evenly. Top with the Pecorino Romano.

7. Bake until the cheese has melted and lightly browned and the sauce is bubbling, about 30 minutes. Let cool on a wire rack for 10 minutes before spooning into serving bowls.

PASTICCIO with BÉCHAMEL AND BOLOGNESE SAUCE PASTICCIO CON BESCIAMELLA E RAGÙ BOLOGNESE

 6 to 8 servings

ROSA TURANO ✳ Pasticcio is northern Italian lasagna. The first time I made it for my Sicilian husband, he said, "This is delicious, but where's the ricotta?" That's the southern way, but we like our lasagna light, with traditional Bolognese ragù, made without herbs, so as not to detract from the pure flavors. Don't neglect the final step of resting the casserole. One of my neighbors, who'd begged for this recipe, skipped it and wound up with lasagna soup. But her kids loved it anyway.

FOR THE RAGÙ
2 tablespoons **olive oil**
1 large **onion**, diced (about 1½ cups)
2 medium **carrots**, diced (about 1 cup)
2 medium **celery** stalks, diced (about 1 cup)
1 tablespoon minced **garlic**

½ pound lean **ground beef**
½ pound **ground veal**
½ pound **ground pork**
1 cup dry **red wine**
1 cup whole **milk**
1 (28-ounce) can crushed **tomatoes**

FOR THE BÉCHAMEL
2½ cups whole **milk**
4 tablespoons (½ stick) unsalted **butter**
¼ cup **all-purpose flour**

½ teaspoon **salt**
½ teaspoon freshly ground **black pepper**

FOR THE CASSEROLE
2 cups **sugo di pomodoro** (page 95) or **plain marinara sauce**
16 fresh **lasagna noodles**, or 12 **no-boil lasagna noodles**

8 ounces **Parmigiano-Reggiano**, finely grated (about 2 cups)
4 tablespoons (½ stick) unsalted **butter**, cut into small pieces

1. To make the ragù, warm the oil in a large pot or Dutch oven set over medium heat. Add the onion, carrots, and celery. Cook, stirring often, until the onion turns golden and soft, about 10 minutes. Add the garlic and cook until fragrant, about 20 seconds.

2. Crumble in the ground beef, veal, and pork and cook, stirring and breaking it up with the back of a wooden spoon, until it's no longer pink, about 7 minutes. Pour in the wine, raise the heat to medium-high, and boil, stirring occasionally, until the wine has been reduced to a thick glaze, about 10 minutes.

3. Pour in the milk and continue boiling, stirring occasionally, until it has also reduced to a glaze, about 10 minutes. Add the tomatoes, stir well, and reduce the heat to very low so the mixture is barely at a simmer. (Once it's at the proper low temperature, you should be able to count the bubbles as they form.) Simmer until very thick and dense, stirring occasionally, about 2 hours. The ragù can be made up to 3 days in advance; cover and refrigerate but bring back to a simmer before continuing with the recipe.

4. To make the béchamel, warm the milk in a small saucepan over low heat just until tiny bubbles fizz around the inside of the pan. Do not boil. Reduce the heat further and keep warm without boiling.

5. Melt the butter in a medium saucepan over medium heat. Whisk in the flour to make a paste. Cook, whisking continuously, for 1 minute to get rid of the raw taste of the flour. Do not brown. Whisk the warm milk into the paste in a slow, steady stream. Cook, whisking continuously, until bubbling, thickened, and smooth, like a hot pudding, about 2 minutes. Whisk in the salt and pepper and set aside, covered, until the ragù is ready.

6. Position the rack in the center of the oven and preheat the oven to 350°F. Stir the béchamel into the thickened ragù until creamy and uniform.

7. To build the casserole, spread 1 cup sugo into the bottom of a 9 x 13-inch baking dish. Overlap 4 lasagna noodles in the dish or set 3 no-boil noodles with ¼-inch gaps between them. Spoon one-third of the ragù on top to make an even coating. Repeat with a second layer of lasagna noodles. Spoon half the remaining ragù on top. Make two more layers using the rest of the ragù. Add a final layer of lasagna noodles, then top with the remaining 1 cup sugo.

8. Cover with parchment paper and seal with aluminum foil. Bake for 20 minutes.

9. Uncover and sprinkle with the Parmigiano-Reggiano and butter. Continue baking, uncovered, until the cheese has melted and browned and the sauce is bubbling, about 20 minutes. Let cool on a wire rack for at least 30 minutes before cutting into squares to serve.

MY PRIZEWINNING MEAT AND THREE-CHEESE LASAGNA WITH EGGPLANT, ASPARAGUS, AND PEAS LASAGNA

8 to 10 servings

TERESA SCALICI ✳ I won two awards for this lasagna—a medal for Best in Staten Island in 2006 and then, two years later, a trophy at the Staten Island Community Resources Center Annual Pasta Bowl. We displayed the trophy in the restaurant for a whole year. So you know it has to be good.

10 tablespoons **olive oil**
1 small **onion**, chopped (about ½ cup)
1 tablespoon minced **garlic**
2 (28-ounce) cans crushed **tomatoes**
1 teaspoon **salt**
½ teaspoon freshly ground **black pepper**
1 pound lean **ground beef**
3 medium Italian **eggplants** (about 2¼ pounds), peeled and diced
½ pound small **white button mushrooms**, thinly sliced
10 thin **asparagus** spears, cut into 1-inch pieces

2 cups frozen **peas**, thawed
5 paper-thin **prosciutto crudo** slices, cut into small pieces
5 thin **speck** slices, cut into small pieces
1 cup whole-milk **ricotta**
1 pound **mozzarella**, shredded (about 4 cups)
4 ounces **Parmigiano-Reggiano,** finely grated (about 1 cup)
16 dried **lasagna noodles**, cooked and drained

1. Warm 2 tablespoons of the oil in a large pot or Dutch oven set over medium heat. Add the onion and cook, stirring often, until softened, about 3 minutes. Add the garlic and cook until it is beginning to brown, about 1 minute. Add the tomatoes, salt, and pepper. Reduce the heat to low and simmer, stirring often, until the tomatoes begin to break down, about 5 minutes.

2. Working in batches, pass the tomato sauce through a food mill into a large bowl. Ladle 1 cup of the tomato sauce into a small bowl, then pour the rest back into the pot. Cover and set aside.

3. Warm 2 tablespoons more oil in a large skillet set over medium heat, then add the ground beef. Cook, breaking up the beef and stirring often, until browned and cooked through, about 8 minutes. Transfer the beef to a colander to drain off any excess fat. Stir the beef into the tomato sauce.

4. Warm 2 tablespoons more oil in the same skillet set over medium-high heat. Add the eggplant; cook, stirring often, until lightly browned, about 10 minutes. Transfer to the colander to drain off any excess fat. Stir the eggplant into the tomato sauce.

5. Warm 2 tablespoons more oil in the skillet set over medium heat. Add the mushrooms and cook, stirring often, until lightly browned and tender, about 8 minutes. Transfer to the colander to drain off any excess fat. Stir the mushrooms into the tomato sauce.

6. Finally, warm the remaining 2 tablespoons oil in the same skillet set over medium heat. Add the asparagus and cook, stirring often, until bright green and al dente, about 4 minutes. Transfer to the colander, drain any excess oil, and stir into the tomato sauce.

7. Stir the peas, prosciutto, and speck into the tomato sauce. Bring to a boil, stirring occasionally, then reduce the heat to low and simmer, stirring once in a while, until slightly thickened, about 15 minutes.

8. Meanwhile, position the rack in the center of the oven and preheat the oven to 350°F. Mix the ricotta, mozzarella, and Parmigiano-Reggiano in a medium bowl.

9. To assemble the lasagna, first ladle ¾ cup of the meat sauce into a small saucepan, cover, and keep warm over very low heat. Spread ½ cup of the meat sauce over the bottom of a 9 x 13-inch baking dish. Overlap 4 lasagna noodles in the baking dish, then spread one-third of the meat sauce over them and crumble one-quarter of the cheese mixture evenly on top. Repeat to make two more layers. Add the remaining lasagna noodles, then top the whole casserole with the reserved plain tomato sauce in the bowl and the remaining cheese mixture.

10. Bake until the cheese has melted and lightly browned and the sauce is bubbling, about 30 minutes. Let cool on a wire rack for 20 minutes. Meanwhile, bring the reserved meat sauce to a simmer over medium-low heat. When you cut the lasagna into squares to serve, drizzle 1 tablespoon of the meat sauce over each helping.

SICILIAN LASAGNA ANELLETTI AL FORNO

 ———————————————————————————— *6 to 8 servings* ⊢———⊣

MARGHERITA AMATO ✳ *Anelletti* are small, flat rings of pasta that are layered like lasagna over a filling of cheese, meats, and sliced eggs.

4 tablespoons (½ stick) unsalted **butter**, cut into very small pieces, plus more for the baking dish
½ cup fresh **breadcrumbs**
2 tablespoons **olive oil**
½ cup chopped red **onion**
1 medium **carrot**, chopped (about ½ cup)
1 medium **celery** stalk, chopped (about ½ cup)
2 tablespoons minced fresh **basil**
½ teaspoon **salt**
½ teaspoon freshly ground **black pepper**

1 cup dry **white wine**
1 (28-ounce) can crushed **tomatoes**
1 cup frozen **peas**, thawed
1 pound dried **anelletti**, cooked until barely tender and drained
2 ounces **Parmigiano-Reggiano**, finely grated (about ½ cup)
8 ounces **mozzarella**, diced
8 ounces **prosciutto cotto** or **boiled deli ham** (do not use prosciutto crudo), diced
3 hard-boiled **eggs**, peeled and sliced

1. Position the rack in the center of the oven and preheat the oven to 350°F. Generously butter a 9 x 13-inch baking dish and sprinkle half the breadcrumbs over the bottom.

2. Warm the oil in a large pot or Dutch oven set over medium heat, then add the onion, carrot, and celery. Cook, stirring occasionally, until the onion has softened, about 5 minutes. Add the basil, salt, and pepper; stir until fragrant, about 30 seconds.

3. Pour in the wine and raise the heat to medium-high. Cook, stirring occasionally, until the liquid has reduced by half, about 10 minutes. Add the tomatoes and peas; cook, stirring often, until slightly thickened, about 5 minutes. Stir in the anelletti and the Parmigiano-Reggiano.

4. Pour half the anelletti mixture into the baking dish and spread it evenly. Sprinkle evenly with the mozzarella, ham, and eggs. Cover with the remaining anelletti mixture and top with the remaining breadcrumbs. Dot with the butter.

5. Bake until the breadcrumbs have browned and the sauce is bubbling, about 25 minutes. Let cool on a wire rack for 10 minutes before spooning into serving bowls.

VIII

PESCE

JODY SCARAVELLA *Both my maternal grandparents, Nonna Domenica and Nonno Gaetano, came from fishing villages—Messina and Sciacca, respectively—so there was always interesting seafood on their table. But my sister, Marianna, really had the touch with delicate cuttlefish or* seppia. *She'd dress it lightly with olive oil, parsley, and a little Parmesan and broil it. I lost Marianna not long after my mother, so I also honor her memory at the Enoteca.*

Elvira Pantaleo

I was born in Palermo, Sicily, into a family of eight children. I was the baby until I was ten—the "walking stick" of my father's old age, he said. But then Silvio, my younger brother, came along to steal my thunder. He was nicknamed the *baronetto*.

At the Sciacca beach, 1963

I was a chile-pepper child, the mischief maker. I'd play a game with my brothers and sisters when we ate Indian figs, or prickly pears, which we all loved. With one of us out of the room, the others would hide a toothpick in one of the fruits. The returning player got to eat prickly pears, one by one, but had to stop at the toothpick. When it was my turn, I got the toothpick in the first bite—no fair! So I kept chewing.

My brothers and sisters were shocked, convinced that I had the toothpick. I kept shaking my head to deny it until they pried open my mouth. There it was, proof that I'd cheated. Just as anyone would have expected me to . . .

We were—and are—a close-knit family. My father, especially, loved to entertain, so our home was where all the friends and relatives gathered. There were rarely fewer than twenty people at our table, and for holidays we'd host forty or fifty. The morning of these parties, my mother used to wake us at dawn to help cook. She was the boss; we just carried out her orders, chopping onions or whatever, laughing like crazy the whole time. If we picked at the food, she'd swat our hands with her wooden spoon—that's what I do with my husband today, when I catch his fingers in the pot. But the whole experience—the preparation, the food, the guests at the table—was joyous. That's why cooking became my life's passion.

Even on normal days, we cooked for lunch and dinner. There was never a "sandwich moment" in our house. My mother, a magnificent cook, made us watch and feel, to learn the process and taste the food, to develop our palates. She also made all her own preserves: jams, *limoncello* (a lemon liqueur), artichokes, eggplants, olives, and, of course, tomatoes and tomato sauce.

Both my parents held strong beliefs about food: chiefly, that the quality of the ingredients is fundamental. We had a country place where we grew fruits and vegetables, raised chickens for eggs, and slaughtered our own pigs to make sausage and ham. For fish, my father went down to the docks to examine the daily catch. He always came home proud, calling out to my mother, "Look, Carmelina! It's alive!" That's how fresh the fish were. Sometimes the fish really were alive, like lobsters with snapping claws. He'd chase us holding one, threatening to pinch us, as we screamed and ran, laughing.

My father was playful that way, loving and good-hearted, though very strict with us when it came to behavior and values. An automotive wizard, he owned a car restoration center, with forty employees doing everything from bodywork to seat upholstery. When the Pope came to Palermo, my father's shop outfitted the papal car—a real honor.

During times when my mother helped my father in the shop, the job of cooking family meals fell to her four daughters. I, the baby, was the only one glad to do it. Not only did I love the responsibility, but I found cooking very creative. Truthfully, one reason it was so creative was that I'd pocket half the money that my mother left for groceries. (I'd use some to bribe Silvio to do my housecleaning chores.) So I always had to scramble, improvising meals from whatever we had in the house.

As a result, I learned to cook so well that Rosario, my husband, proposed after tasting my *spezzatino di manzo*, a long-simmered beef stew. In Italian, there's an expression, "*L'uomo si prende per la gola*," which is the same as the American one, "The way to a man's heart is through his stomach." On either side of the ocean, it can happen. My marriage to Rosario has lasted thirty happy years.

I wasn't sure that I ever wanted to get married. I was twenty-nine years old, living very happily in my parents' house, and running an auto insurance bureau. Rosario had a collision—not his fault—and was owed an insurance payment. We paid claims on Tuesdays, so I told him to come then, not realizing that I was missing some paperwork. Apologizing, I asked him to return the following week. Rosario agreed—and then sent a huge bouquet of roses, with a card inviting me to dinner.

Of course, I was flattered by the gesture,

With my dad, 1960

but being a little mischievous, I said no. "Let's just have an *aperitivo* then," Rosario insisted. "Just a drink before dinner." He suggested a place that I passed on my way home, so I agreed. But I brought along my own insurance—my brother Silvio.

The evening was pleasant enough. Rosario followed up with twenty-one red roses. I thanked him, saying, "No more." But another bouquet arrived, and then another— every day, twenty-one long-stemmed red roses showed up at my office.

"Who is this guy?" I had to wonder. "A millionaire?"

As it turned out, Rosario was a florist.

We dated for a couple of months. We were at a disco one night—I love to dance, but he hates it—when Rosario declared, "I love you."

"Don't say that," I told him. "You don't even know me."

But he believed he did, enough to invite me to dinner on February 12, his birthday. Knowing that Rosario woke up early to get his flowers from the market, I quickly calculated that I'd be home by eleven, in time to go out partying with my friends. But after dinner, Rosario suggested going dancing. I couldn't tell him that I'd made plans, so I pretended that my stomach was killing me. Very concerned, he drove me home, where I raced to Mondello, the beach that had all the best parties.

The next day Rosario called to check on me. "I drank some tea and went to bed," I said, weakly. "Then why was your car parked at the Mondello beach?" he asked. "What . . . my car?" "Yes, and here's what you were wearing. . . ." I was caught.

After that, I promised to go out only with Rosario. Then, one weekend, when he was on a trip to Rome, I hooked up with friends for a wild night out. In the wee hours, when I was pulling up to the house, I saw a car's headlights flashing. Rosario had been parked there all night, waiting. He'd never gone out of town.

Just to make this even more of a Sicilian story, in the fight that followed, I whipped my head around and somehow smacked him in the face, blackening his eye. But we made up and, within a few months, decided to marry.

In those days, weddings were typically held at restaurants. But Rosario suggested holding it at my family's country place, where my parents, now retired, were living full-time. They loved the idea. My father built two fire pits, each fifteen feet long, one for meat and the other for fish. Hired cooks would grill to order whatever food a guest requested. There were also separate seafood stations for octopus, clams and mussels, oysters, sea urchins, and inky cuttlefish; plus one for bread and spleen, a local specialty. One long table was full of Sicilian favorites, like

Family and friends at my brother Silvio's birthday, 1965

eggplant and artichokes cooked all different ways; cardoons; and *babbaluci*, or escargot, in big copper pots. Fresh fruits were heaped in a classic Sicilian *carretto*, a brightly painted, two-wheeled donkey cart, with storytelling images. It was a magnificent feast for all the senses.

My father had posted banners on the road, reading: *If You Want to Eat Well, Come Celebrate with Rosario and Elvira.* That's how a crew of American tourists stumbled onto us, thinking they were going to a restaurant. But my father welcomed them, saying, "Stay and eat whatever you want." They left a stack of American dollars as a wedding gift.

In time, we were blessed with our greatest gift: Alessandro, our son.

I always loved to work, so once we were married, I joined forces with Rosario. One day, at the flower fair, he and I met an acquaintance who wanted to open a banquet hall. We steered him to a space next to our flower shop, and he invited us to become his partners. That's when it struck me that I actually had a strong culinary vision. I didn't like high-end restaurants because the food fashionable at the time was so fussy, supposedly sophisticated. Only at simple places did they serve the more typical Sicilian food that I grew up on and loved to cook.

I was excited to start a business focused on traditional food. The partnership soured, so Rosario and I bought the other guy out, determined to go it alone. We knew nothing about running a restaurant, so we hired a top staff, from experienced waiters to an exceptional chef. Unlike other banquet halls, which had standardized menus, we created a customized feast for each event. The strategy paid off, and pretty soon we were hosting the best parties in Palermo.

When Alessandro reached high school age, he'd pitch in, washing dishes, bussing tables, and pouring wine. He worked his way up to second in command, right below the headwaiter, with no special breaks. At work, he called me signora instead of Mama, and his colleagues would always say, "You're just like rest of us"—meaning he never had the attitude of an owners' son. For fifteen years, our business thrived.

Change in life is inevitable. Our lives changed when Alessandro went to America on vacation and wound up staying. In 2010, I came to visit for one month and stayed for three. At the time, Alessandro was trying to start his own business, so I called Rosario to say, "I can't leave him now."

In my culture, the family is everything, the center of the universe. If my only son were in Australia, France—anywhere—that's where I'd want to be. Rosario felt the same way. So we closed the business and moved to New York to start a new adventure.

We settled in Bensonhurst, Brooklyn, where there are plenty of Italian-speakers. Rosario worked in a friend's bar, which had an Italian clientele. He learned a few English phrases and tried to teach me, saying, "Think of the Sicilian word for 'mother,' *mamach*—well, that's how you say 'how much?'" Alessandro, who speaks good English—he's young—married an Italian American woman whose family spent many years in Italy, so she's fluent in both languages.

I'm the one who struggles to navigate the English-speaking world. I feel at home at the Enoteca because the Italian brands are familiar, but I wish I could interact more with the customers. I recognize the words "good" and "delicious," and once a group asked me to autograph their menu. That made me feel so prized.

Sometimes I make an impression, like the time when a family who owned a car service and spoke some Italian came for dinner. Thanks to my automotive background, we had a lively chat. When they asked how I'd get home, I explained that I'd meet Rosario at the bar and together we'd take a car service. Well, when I got to the bar, outside, idling, was a huge stretch limousine. Rosario was peering out the door, trying to see which dignitary was coming to drink in a neighborhood place. Then the driver came in and asked for me by name. My moment of glory!

I rode home like a queen. The driver said, "No charge," and I tipped him $10. Of course, a car service would have cost me only $6, but it was worth it.

My one handicap in America is not speaking English. It frustrates me to death because I'm opinionated. So when I learn, look out! I have a lot to tell the world.

FISH SOUP PALERMO STYLE

ZUPPA DI PESCE ALLA PALERMITANA

 6 servings ┣━━┫

ELVIRA PANTALEO ✳ You can substitute snapper, grouper, scrod, haddock, or sea bass for the cod in this classic soup, a one-pot meal.

3 tablespoons **olive oil**, plus more for serving
1 small **onion**, chopped (about ½ cup)
3 **garlic** cloves
1 cup dry **white wine**
2½ pounds **beefsteak tomatoes**, peeled, seeded, cored, and diced (see page 57)
¼ cup minced fresh **flat-leaf parsley**
6 cups **fish broth**
½ teaspoon **salt**
½ teaspoon **red pepper flakes**, or to taste
¼ teaspoon **saffron**

½ pound small **cherrystone clams**, scrubbed
½ pound **squid**, cleaned and cut into ½-inch-thick rings or frozen **calamari rings**, thawed
1 pound **cod**, skin removed and flesh cut into 2-inch pieces
½ pound **mussels**, scrubbed and debearded
½ pound medium **shrimp** (about 30 per pound), peeled and deveined
6 slices **Italian bread**, toasted

1. Warm the oil in a large pot or Dutch oven set over medium heat, then add the onion and garlic. Cook, stirring often, until they both begin to brown, about 10 minutes. Add the wine and scrape up any browned bits from the bottom of the pot as it comes to a simmer.

2. Add the tomatoes and parsley. Return to a boil, then reduce the heat to low and simmer, stirring occasionally, until the tomatoes begin to break down, about 10 minutes. Stir in the broth, salt, red pepper flakes, and saffron. Cover and cook, stirring occasionally, until the tomatoes have broken down into a soup, about 20 minutes.

3. Stir in the clams and squid; cook for 4 minutes. Stir in the cod, mussels, and shrimp. Cover and simmer without stirring (to preserve the fish and shellfish), until the clams and mussels have opened, about 10 minutes. Discard the garlic cloves and any mollusks that do not open.

4. Place a slice of bread in each bowl. Ladle the soup over the bread and drizzle with oil.

SAUTÉED CUTTLEFISH OR BABY SQUID

SEPPIA O CALAMARETTI MURATI

 4 servings

ELVIRA PANTALEO ✳ This traditional preparation of wine, onions, and tomato paste is delicious with either baby cuttlefish or baby squid. Look for cuttlefish or squid no more than about three inches long. If you buy them from a fish market, ask to have them cleaned. If you buy them frozen, they will be ready to use.

4 tablespoons **olive oil**

2 medium **onions**, halved and cut into thin half-moons

2 **garlic** cloves, unpeeled

2 pounds tiny **cuttlefish** or **baby squid**, cleaned and rinsed

1 cup dry **white wine**

1½ tablespoons **tomato paste**

1 teaspoon **red pepper flakes**, or to taste

¼ teaspoon **salt**

¼ teaspoon freshly ground **black pepper**

Minced fresh **flat-leaf parsley**, for garnish

1. Warm the oil in a deep skillet set over medium-low heat. Add the onions and garlic; cook, stirring often, until the onions are golden brown, about 15 minutes.

2. Discard the garlic cloves. Add the cuttlefish; cook for 2 minutes, stirring continuously, to coat in the onions. Pour in ½ cup of the wine, raise the heat to medium, and bring to a simmer. Cook, stirring often, until the wine has reduced to a thick glaze, about 5 minutes.

3. Add the remaining ½ cup wine, the tomato paste, red pepper flakes, salt, pepper, and ½ cup water, and stir until the tomato paste dissolves. Cover, reduce the heat, and simmer, stirring occasionally, until the cuttlefish are tender, about 15 minutes. Turn off the heat and set aside, covered, for 15 minutes before serving. Garnish with parsley.

STUFFED CALAMARI CALAMARI RIPIENI

 6 servings as a starter or 4 as a main course

CHRISTINA NARISI CARROZZA ✳ Calamari stuffed with sausage is one of my signature dishes.

1½ pounds small **squid** (each about 4 inches long), cleaned
3 tablespoons **olive oil**
4 teaspoons minced **garlic**
8 ounces mild **Italian sausage**, casings removed
½ cup dry **white wine**
½ cup fresh **breadcrumbs**

2 ounces **Parmigiano-Reggiano**, finely grated (about ½ cup)
2 tablespoons minced fresh **flat-leaf parsley**
1 (28-ounce) can crushed **tomatoes**
½ cup packed fresh **basil**, minced
¼ teaspoon **salt**
¼ teaspoon freshly ground **black pepper**

1. Remove the tentacles from the squid bodies. Finely chop the tentacles.

2. Warm 2 tablespoons of the oil in a deep skillet set over medium heat. Add 2 teaspoons of the garlic. Cook, stirring often, until lightly browned, about 1 minute. Crumble in the sausage and add the tentacles. Cook, stirring often and breaking up the sausage with the back of a wooden spoon, until the sausage has browned, about 7 minutes.

3. Pour in the wine, raise the heat to medium high, and cook, stirring often, until the wine has reduced to a thick glaze, about 5 minutes. Remove from the heat; stir in the breadcrumbs, Parmigiano-Reggiano, and parsley. Scrape the sausage mixture into a bowl and let cool to room temperature, about 30 minutes.

4. Meanwhile, clean and dry the pan and set it over medium heat. Add the remaining 1 tablespoon oil as well as the remaining 2 teaspoons garlic. Stir until lightly browned, about 2 minutes. Stir in the tomatoes, basil, salt, and pepper; bring to a boil, then reduce the heat to very low and simmer, stirring occasionally, for 20 minutes.

5. As the sauce simmers, stuff each squid body with 2 tablespoons of the sausage mixture. Pinch the opening of each squid body closed and secure it with a toothpick.

6. When the sauce has simmered for 20 minutes, add the stuffed calamari. Cover and continue simmering until tender, about 20 minutes. Remove from the heat for 20 minutes to let the calamari rest and the flavors blend before serving.

SICILIAN-STYLE SALT COD WITH RAISINS, TOMATOES, AND OLIVES BACCALÀ ALLA SICILIANA

 4 servings

TERESA SCALICI ✳ This is the traditional Sicilian preparation for *baccalà* with my nonna's additions: tomatoes and black olives. If you like, you can serve the dish over cooked ziti or penne.

1 pound **baccalà** (salt cod)
3 tablespoons **olive oil**
1 tablespoon minced **garlic**
1 (28-ounce) can crushed **tomatoes**
½ cup **raisins**

½ cup **pine nuts**
⅓ cup pitted **black olives**
¼ cup **nonpareil capers** in brine, drained
  and rinsed

1. Put the baccalà in a large bowl, cover with cold water, and refrigerate for 24 hours, changing the water twice. Drain, then break the cod into four equal pieces.

2. Warm the oil in a deep skillet set over medium heat. Add the garlic; cook, stirring often, until lightly browned, about 1 minute. Add the tomatoes, raisins, pine nuts, olives, capers, and ⅓ cup water. Bring to a boil, then reduce the heat to medium-low and cook, stirring occasionally, until the tomatoes begin to break down into a sauce, about 10 minutes.

3. Add the baccalà. Cover and simmer until the fish flakes when pricked with a fork, about 30 minutes. Serve in bowls.

EELS IN WINE AND GARLIC SAUCE

ANGUILLA AL VINO E AGLIO

 4 *servings*

FRANCESCA LEONE ✳ My father loved to fish, so eels were often on our table. This dish was one of the essentials for our Christmas Eve dinner. Let the fishmonger clean and skin the eels for you.

4 (1-pound) **eels**, cleaned, skin removed, and flesh cut into 2-inch pieces
1 tablespoon fresh **lemon juice**
½ teaspoon **salt**
2 cups **all-purpose flour**, for dredging
4 tablespoons **olive oil**
1½ tablespoons minced **garlic**, or to taste

2 medium red **onions**, halved and cut into thin half-moons
4 **bay leaves**
1 cup dry **white wine**
Torn fresh **flat-leaf parsley**, for garnish
Freshly ground **black pepper**, for garnish

1. Toss the eel pieces with the lemon juice and salt in a large bowl. Lay the eel on a large baking sheet to dry, about 10 minutes.

2. Spread the flour on a large plate. Dredge the eel pieces in the flour, shaking off any excess so each has a very light coating. Set aside on a cutting board or baking sheet.

3. Warm the oil in a deep skillet set over medium heat. Add the garlic and cook, stirring often, until golden brown, about 2 minutes. Add the onions, bay leaves, and eel pieces; toss very gently over the heat to combine. Pour the wine over everything.

4. Raise the heat to medium-high and bring to a boil. Cook, without disturbing, until the wine has reduced by about half, about 5 minutes. Cover, reduce the heat, and simmer until the eel is cooked through but the onions are still a little firm, about 10 minutes. Remove and discard the bay leaves. Serve in bowls, garnished with parsley and pepper.

SICILIAN-STYLE TUNA FILLETS WITH ONIONS AND VINEGAR TONNO CON LA CIPUDDATA

4 servings

ELVIRA PANTALEO ✳ Honey and vinegar add piquancy to this cool summery dish.

1 cup **all-purpose flour**, for dredging
4 (6-ounce) **tuna fillets**
⅔ cup **olive oil**
4 medium **onions**, halved and cut into thin half-moons

5 tablespoons **red wine vinegar**
¼ cup **honey**
½ teaspoon **salt**
½ teaspoon freshly ground **black pepper**
Torn fresh **mint**, for garnish

1. Spread the flour on a large plate. Dredge the tuna in the flour, coating all sides (including the edges). Shake off any excess and set the tuna on a cutting board.

2. Warm the oil in a deep skillet set over medium heat. Slip in the tuna. Fry, turning once, until golden, about 6 minutes for medium-rare or 9 minutes for cooked through. Transfer to a serving platter.

3. Add the onions to the skillet, reduce the heat to medium-low, and cook, stirring often, until deep gold, about 20 minutes. Stir in the vinegar, honey, salt, and pepper. Raise the heat to medium and cook for 1 minute to reduce slightly.

4. Pour the onion sauce over the tuna and garnish with mint. Cover loosely with plastic wrap and refrigerate for 20 minutes to blend the flavors. Serve cool.

BRANZINO IN A SALT CRUST WITH LEMON AND OREGANO SAUCE

BRANZINO IN CROSTA DI SALE AL SALMORIGLIO

4 servings

ELVIRA PANTALEO ✳ *Salmoriglio*, a simple sauce made with fresh oregano, can be served with meat or vegetables but is especially good with fish. Its name, which has many variant spellings in Sicilian, is a combination of the words for salt (*sale*), lemon (*limone*), and oregano (*origano*).

FOR THE FISH

4 pounds coarse **sea salt**, or more as needed

2 whole **branzino**, gutted but not scaled

4 fresh **thyme** sprigs

4 fresh **parsley** sprigs

2 **garlic** cloves, halved

FOR THE SAUCE

½ cup extra-virgin **olive oil**

⅓ cup fresh **lemon juice**

2 tablespoons minced fresh **oregano**

¼ teaspoon **salt**

¼ teaspoon freshly ground **black pepper**

1. Position the rack in the center of the oven and preheat the oven to 400°F. Overlap three 32-inch-long sheets of aluminum foil crosswise in a 9 x 13-inch baking dish. Spread a ½-inch layer of sea salt across the bottom of the baking dish.

2. Stuff the cavity of each fish with 2 thyme sprigs, 2 parsley sprigs, and 2 garlic clove halves. Lay the fish side by side on the sea salt in the baking dish. Pour the rest of the sea salt over the fish to cover them completely. (The scales protect the fish from getting too salty.) Fold the foil over the fish and seal tightly, making sure no air can escape from any seam. Bake for 30 minutes.

3. To make the sauce, whisk the oil, lemon juice, oregano, salt, and pepper in a small bowl.

4. Transfer the baking dish with the fish to a wire rack to cool for 5 minutes, then unwrap the foil. Tap with a wooden spoon to crack the crust; gently remove the salt crust, revealing the fish below. Using a large spatula, transfer the fish to a cutting board. Carefully peel off the skin, taking care that no scales fall onto the meat. Gently pull the meat off the bones and transfer to serving plates. Drizzle with the sauce to serve.

STUFFED SWORDFISH ROLLS

INVOLTINI DI PESCE SPADA

4 servings

ELVIRA PANTALEO ※ Swordfish fillets are rolled up around a filling in this elegant dish. Ask the fish market to slice the swordfish to the recommended weight and thickness.

FOR THE FILLING

2 tablespoons **olive oil**, plus more
 for the baking dish
1¾ cups fresh **breadcrumbs**
¼ pound small **shrimp** (about 40 per
 pound), peeled, deveined, and chopped
2 ounces skinless **swordfish**, minced
1 small **plum tomato**, finely chopped

3 tablespoons fresh **lemon juice**
2 tablespoons minced fresh **flat-leaf
 parsley**
1 teaspoon minced **garlic**
½ teaspoon **salt**
½ teaspoon freshly ground **black pepper**

FOR THE CASSEROLE

8 (2-ounce) skinless **swordfish fillets**,
 each no more than ¼ inch thick
2 small **plum tomatoes**, cut into ¼-inch-
 thick rounds

¼ cup fresh **breadcrumbs**
4 tablespoons **olive oil**
Torn fresh **basil** leaves, for garnish

1. Position the rack in the center of the oven and preheat the oven to 375°F. Lightly oil a 9 x 13-inch baking dish.

2. To make the filling, mix 2 tablespoons of the oil, the breadcrumbs, shrimp, swordfish, tomato, lemon juice, parsley, garlic, salt, and pepper in a large bowl until moistened and a little pasty.

3. To make the casserole, lay each swordfish fillet on a clean work surface. Lay ⅓ cup of the filling in a line about ½ inch away from the longest edge. Roll closed, starting with the edge nearest to the filling. Place seam side down in the baking dish.

4. Tuck the tomato slices between the rolls. Sprinkle with the breadcrumbs and drizzle with oil. Bake until the breadcrumbs are lightly browned and the fish is cooked through, 10 to 12 minutes. Let cool in the baking dish for 5 minutes before serving warm in bowls, with basil and any pan juices drizzled over the top.

BREAM IN POTATO CRUST

ORATA IN CROSTA DI PATATE

4 servings

ELVIRA PANTALEO ✳ *Orata is a fish prized in European cooking. Gilt-head bream is a variety available at well-stocked fish markets in North America, or you can substitute porgy, red snapper, or sea bass in this recipe.*

4 **orata** or **gilt-head breams**, cleaned and scaled, heads removed
8 (4-inch) fresh **parsley** sprigs, plus more for garnish
6 (4-inch) fresh **rosemary** sprigs
8 **bay leaves**
6 **garlic** cloves
3 tablespoons fresh **lemon juice**, plus more for serving

½ teaspoon **salt**
½ teaspoon freshly ground **black pepper**
1 cup dry **white wine**
4 tablespoons **olive oil**
6 medium white **potatoes** (about 2 pounds), peeled and sliced about ⅛ inch thick
2 medium **plum tomatoes**, cut into 8 wedges each

1. Position the rack in the center of the oven and preheat the oven to 400°F.

2. Stuff the cavity of each fish with 2 parsley sprigs, 1 rosemary sprig, 1 bay leaf, and 1 garlic clove. Drizzle the fish inside and out with the lemon juice, along with a sprinkle of salt and pepper. Press the edges to close the opening.

3. Pour ½ cup of the wine into a small roasting pan that will hold the 4 fish in one layer. Stir in 2 tablespoons of the oil as well as ½ cup water. Overlap half the potato slices in the liquid. Add the remaining 2 rosemary sprigs, remaining 4 bay leaves, and remaining 2 garlic cloves. Set the fish on top of the potatoes; arrange the remainder of the potatoes over and around the fish. Set the tomatoes on top of the potatoes. Pour the remaining ½ cup wine and 2 tablespoons oil over everything.

4. Bake for 10 minutes. Reduce the oven temperature to 375°F and continue baking until the potatoes are golden and the fish is cooked through, about 20 minutes. To serve, remove and discard the bay leaves and divide the fish and potatoes among serving plates; drizzle with the pan juices. Garnish with parsley and drizzle with more lemon juice before serving.

← IX →

CARNE

JODY SCARAVELLA *Since southern Italy has so much coastline, families like my mother's ate far more fish and pasta than they did meat, which was costly. The north is more into agriculture and animal husbandry. So now, thanks to the nonnas, I've been learning a new vocabulary of Italian cuisine.*

Christina Narisi Carrozza

I'll never forget the day I arrived in New York. As our ship, the *Raffaello*, docked, the grayness overwhelmed me—the industrial wasteland of Manhattan's West Side, the smog, the sunless sky. As two of my uncles drove us to Howard Beach, Queens, where they lived, all I could see was urban decay. It was 1973, and the city was going bankrupt.

With my mother and younger sister, 1963

At seventeen, I was too young to stay in Italy on my own but old enough to be afraid of such a gritty and dangerous-looking city. I'd come from Bergamo, a beautiful walled city at the foothills of the Alps, ringed by little farms, twenty-five miles from Milan. We lived in an apartment, with my father's mother upstairs and my aunt on the first floor. We were a close-knit, loving family community—eating together, cooking together, playing music together. Now, though we shared a connecting wall with my mother's brother, we were adrift—my parents, Luciano and Domenica; my younger brother, Giuseppe; my sister, Isidora; and me—as a solitary unit.

Most isolating was the fact that I didn't speak English, and the ethnic Italians in Queens, including my relatives, spoke dialect. For a long time, I felt like a deaf person in a crowded room, observing but unable to participate because I couldn't understand or communicate.

I had to work, though. The first time I rode the subway alone, heading to hairdressing school in downtown Brooklyn, I got lost. Luckily, a kind stranger recognized the address on the business card I was clutching and redirected me. But I persisted, and every day, I grew a little more independent. In less than a year, I got my hairdressing license.

I apprenticed at a tiny Brooklyn salon where the owner spoke Italian. I'd get there at 7:30 in the morning, planning to grab a coffee, only to find our eight o'clock customers—little old ladies in babushkas—huddled by the door. I'd have to duck around the corner before they saw me. And the hairstyles they expected—huge teased bubbles, shellacked with hairspray so they barely moved! I'd never seen hair like that before.

At night I'd cry to my mother and aunt, "Why are we still here? Why can't we go home?" They were always encouraging and patient. "Don't worry," they'd say.

"You're working. You'll meet all different people. You're going to have a new life here, a better life."

And, of course, that's what happened.

My mother was no stranger to change. Coming to America was her second uprooting. She and my father were Sicilian, and I was born in San Giuseppe Jato, a mountain village outside Palermo. Big families were the norm—my mother had eight siblings and my father, seven—which meant lots of mouths to feed in a fairly impoverished area. When I was three, my father's family—parents, children plus spouses (including my mother), and grandkids—picked up and moved to Bergamo, in the more prosperous, industrial north.

My grandfather, a cobbler who'd made boots for the army during World War II, opened a shoe-repair shop with my father, who also worked in a textile firm. My mother, trained as a seamstress, couldn't find work, so she became an elderly woman's caregiver. Her paycheck was critical because, when I was nine, my father got a serious lung ailment, requiring surgery. It left him weakened, with a huge, frightening scar.

Being the oldest, I then got new responsibilities—caring for my brother and sister and doing the daily cooking. My mother would show me what to do— say, to make *polpettone*, or meat loaf with salsa verde, by mixing pork, veal, and beef, then poaching the meat loaf in boiling water. If I needed help, my aunt and nonna were right there in the building.

My earliest childhood memory is of my nonna making tomato sauce. I'm tiny—probably three or four years old—sitting on a step stool, watching, and in my mind the smells are just as vivid as the sights. She starts by sautéing a lot of finely chopped onions in a little butter and olive oil, then grinds her tomatoes in a food mill before adding them to the pan. As the sauce comes together, she throws in some salt, pepper, and fresh basil. That was it—so simple and so delicious that I would practically lick my plate.

It was my beloved uncle Giovanni who taught me to make lasagna with béchamel and Bolognese sauce. That was unusual, first because he was a man, when mostly women were in the kitchen, and second because the béchamel version (as opposed to the kind with ricotta) comes from the north. My mother cooked Sicilian-style, as she'd been taught, but our neighbors in Bergamo had a different approach to food.

Growing up, I had the best of both worlds, food-wise. Northern and southern Italy are two extremes, two completely different cultures. Southern Italy is all about fish—being surrounded by water, that's what it had; while the north, with mountains and grazing land, has more livestock like pigs, cows, and sheep, so its menus are full of pork, veal, and lamb. You see mostly pasta in the south, while the north also has polenta and risotto. In the south, you'll get stuffed manicotti and lasagna with ricotta; in the north, it's cannelloni, filled with meat, and lasagna with béchamel. Southerners use Pecorino Romano, which is sharper and saltier than the northern favorite, Parmesan. In cooking, I'd say southerners probably use 90 percent olive oil, while in the north, there's more butter, pancetta, and lard.

The north is colder, so the herbs are different. Basil, parsley, and oregano are common in the south—I never saw anyone use oregano in the north. There, it was more rosemary, sage, bay leaves, and nutmeg. It's my impression that northerners use more onions and southerners more garlic. Different vegetables, too: There are wintery, pumpkin-y squashes up north, regular broccoli, and Swiss chard, while in the south you'll see the more bitter broccoli rabe.

At least, these are the differences I've observed. Of course, like everything else, they're fading now that we have supermarkets, refrigeration, the Internet—today people cook everything. But what I hope will never fade are the food rituals uniting families, which were all-important when I was young.

Take the holiday traditions. For New Year's Eve, we always had sausages and pizzas or, better yet, a delicious pork roast that I still make, with oranges and lard. For Easter, there was always roast lamb with sage and rosemary. And for birthdays, my nonna would make each of us her special cake, which was actually ladyfingers layered with panna cotta, with a sprinkling of cinnamon and shaved chocolate on top. That was an incredible treat.

After those festive meals, everyone would gather around my nonna's table. One of my uncles would strum his guitar, and everyone sang. Such beautiful voices! My uncle Giovanni and uncle Carmelo, who still lives in Bergamo, would break into "Mama," the classic that every Italian singer—Pavarotti, Bocelli,

My father with a fellow soldier, 1959

even Connie Francis—has performed. Written in wartime as the song of soldiers, it chills me to listen to the words about returning to the warmth of a mother's love: "Mama, I am very happy / Because I am returning to you . . . / Mama, I am very happy / Why should we live apart? . . . / Today, your white head / I want to hold tight to my heart." My grandfather would be grinning, proud of his sons, and my nonna would be sobbing and laughing at the same time. Beautiful memories.

More than anything, it was that cocoon of big-family warmth that I missed in America, especially since I was at the age to start a family of my own. How would I even find a mate, being so isolated and lost? My parents were Old World strict, so casual dating wasn't an option. Work and school were the only reasons I was ever allowed to leave the house. So it took some scheming for my friend Maria to fix me up with the brother of the guy she was dating. Amazingly, my parents fell for the story we cooked up. Equally amazing, I fell for the guy.

My English was still sketchy, and he barely spoke Italian (though his parents did). Still, sparks flew—enough that, within months, we got engaged. I was almost nineteen when we married, settling in Bensonhurst, Brooklyn—a blessing because most of the shopkeepers there spoke Italian. For our first anniversary, my new husband gave me a grandfather clock, which I cherished. I guess we weren't thinking about kids when we bought our first couch—white!—but a year and a half later, my daughter, Maria Christina, came along, followed by Carmelo, my son.

Now that I had my own family, I began re-creating my lost world, cooking for all the big celebrations. Everyone came—aunts and uncles, siblings and spouses, cousins, children, friends, and any straggler who, God forbid, was facing a holiday alone. Cooking for thirty or forty was never a burden for me—it was like therapy.

One of my most cherished memories relates to Christmas Eve dinner. It was our most anticipated holiday meal, all fish, according to tradition. The highlight was pasta with fish sauce, made with crabs, shrimp, calamari, mussels, clams, and more. My kids were young, but even with my mother lending a hand, I was getting a little frantic juggling them and trying to clean the fish for the sauce. Then my father said, "Don't worry. I can help."

It was as if time stood still for a second. Then there he was, scrubbing the shellfish, peeling the shrimp. My mother couldn't get over it. Apart from my uncle Giovanni, no man of that generation would ever set foot in the kitchen. Back then, men were waited on, first by their mothers and then by their wives. Yet my father helped that Christmas, which, as it turned out, was his last one on earth.

To me, cooking was a family ritual. I never saw it as a possible career. But now it's become my life. It was my mother who spotted the ad for nonnas in *America Oggi*. I was hired on the spot. My first couple of shifts were absolute terror! It wasn't till the end of the night, with everyone

Me (right) making my First Holy Communion in Bergamo, 1963

assuring me that the food was just fine—even delicious—that I dared to breathe.

But my greatest sense of success—as a cook and as a human being—comes from the way my kids uphold our traditions. Even my son, who I never realized was paying attention. Now he's engaged and cooks for his fiancée Kristen's family on holidays. He's quizzed me about my fish sauce but makes his own variation, which I hope he'll teach me. The same with my eggplant. He says, "Oh, I don't make it your way anymore. I do this and that instead . . ." That doesn't offend me at all—it's a compliment.

Maria Christina has two little girls, Ava Maria and Emily Rose, who are my angels. Since they live in New Jersey, I always stay a few days when I visit. Our favorite thing to do is make pizza. When we make the dough, I'll assign them jobs, like, "Ava, get Nonna the flour," "Emily, sprinkle the yeast in the water," then let them both have the fun of squishing it together, so they get the feel.

Just as I did, they're learning by doing. But our sessions teach more than just how to make pizza—things like cooperation, patience, gentleness, the thrill of accomplishment. But what matters to me is that they're living a tradition stretching back to my nonna and beyond. To me that's the foundation, the most basic essence of who we are.

STUFFED SPLEEN MILZA RIPIENA

8 servings

NINA PICARIELLO ※ In Italy, no part of an animal is ever wasted, and this is a traditional and delicious way to prepare the spleen. It's covered with a membrane that can be chewy; if you prefer a more uniform texture, ask the butcher to remove it.

1 **beef spleen** (about 2 pounds)
4 cups fresh **breadcrumbs**
½ cup packed fresh **flat-leaf parsley**, minced
½ cup mixed **dried fruit**, such as apricots, pitted prunes, pitted dates, and stemmed figs, finely chopped
4 ounces **salami**, casings removed and meat diced

3 large **egg yolks**, lightly beaten
2 tablespoons **nonpareil capers** in brine, drained
½ teaspoon **salt**
½ teaspoon freshly ground **black pepper**
3 tablespoons **olive oil**
1 tablespoon minced **garlic**
1 cup moderately dry **white wine**

1. Place the spleen in a large pot, add water to cover, and bring to a boil. Cover and cook for 15 minutes. Transfer the spleen to a cutting board, and let cool for 20 minutes.

2. Place the breadcrumbs in a large bowl and stir in 2 cups water. Soak for 10 minutes, then gently squeeze handfuls of the breadcrumbs to remove the water. Place the moist breadcrumbs in a large bowl; stir in the parsley, dried fruit, salami, egg yolks, capers, ¼ teaspoon of the salt, and ¼ teaspoon of the pepper.

3. Starting at the longest, thickest side, cut a long, thin slit down the side of the spleen and then deepen the slit to form a pocket by sawing back and forth.

4. Stuff the breadcrumb mixture into the pocket. Thread a sterilized trussing or tapestry needle with a three-foot length of butcher's twine; knot one end. Sew the pocket closed, trimming off excess twine and knotting the twine's other end to seal.

5. Warm the oil in a large skillet set over medium heat, then add the garlic. Cook until lightly browned, stirring often, about 1 minute. Add the spleen and brown on both sides, about 5 minutes. Pour in the wine; stir in the remaining ¼ teaspoon salt and ¼ teaspoon pepper. Bring to a boil, cover, reduce the heat, and simmer until tender, about 1½ hours. Transfer the spleen to a cutting board; let cool for 10 minutes. Carve into ½-inch-thick slices and serve with any remaining pan juices.

QUAIL WITH FRIED PANCETTA AND OLIVES

QUAGLIA CON PANCETTA FRITTA E OLIVE

 2 servings (can be doubled)

FRANCESCA LEONE ✳ Because my mother disapproved of my father's hunting, she wouldn't eat quail. So this is my grandmother's recipe, which the rest of us enjoyed. If you can't find smoked pancetta, which is available at most Italian markets, regular pancetta (along with an ounce of smoked American bacon, if you like) is fine.

2 bone-in **quail** (about 5½ ounces each), cleaned, preferably with feet attached
¼ teaspoon **salt**
¼ teaspoon freshly ground **black pepper**
1 **garlic** clove, halved
1 (4-inch) fresh **rosemary** sprig, halved

8 small fresh **sage** leaves
4 tablespoons **olive oil**
4 paper-thin slices smoked **pancetta**
1 cup dry **white wine**
12 pitted **green olives**

1. Season the quail inside and out with salt and pepper. Stuff each quail with a piece of garlic, a piece of rosemary, and 2 sage leaves.

2. Warm the oil in a deep skillet set over medium heat. Add the pancetta. Fry until crisp, turning once, about 2 minutes. Transfer to a cutting board or plate.

3. Set the quail in the skillet. Brown well, turning once, about 8 minutes. Stir in the wine, olives, and remaining 4 sage leaves. Cover, reduce the heat to low, and cook until the quail are tender at the bone, about 20 minutes. Transfer the quail to a serving platter. Drizzle with the pan juices and garnish with the fried pancetta.

DRUNKEN CHICKEN POLLO UMBRIACO

4 servings

CHRISTINA NARISI CARROZZA ✳ Earthy and colorful, this dish is especially satisfying in cool weather. My family loves it made with either chicken or rabbit.

2 medium white **onions**, halved and cut into thin half-moons
2 small red **onions**, halved and cut into thin half-moons
1 cup **all-purpose flour**, for dredging
1 (4-pound) **chicken**, cut in 8 pieces, giblets and neck removed
8 tablespoons (1 stick) unsalted **butter**
3 tablespoons **olive oil**

2 cups dry **red wine**
2 ounces dried **porcini mushrooms** (about 1 cup soaked)
¼ teaspoon **salt**
¼ teaspoon freshly ground **black pepper**
Classic Polenta (page 81), for serving
Finely grated **Parmigiano-Reggiano**, for garnish

1. Position the rack in the center of the oven and preheat the oven to 375°F. Scatter the onions in an even layer in a 9 x 13-inch baking dish.

2. Spread the flour on a large plate. Dredge the chicken pieces in the flour, coating all sides evenly and shaking off any excess. Set aside.

3. Melt 4 tablespoons of the butter in the oil in a large skillet set over medium heat. Working in batches, brown the chicken until golden, turning once, about 8 minutes per batch. As the chicken is done, transfer it to the baking dish on top of the onions.

4. Pour the wine over the chicken. Cover the baking dish with aluminum foil and bake until the chicken is tender at the bone, about 1 hour.

5. Meanwhile, set the porcini in a small heatproof bowl, cover with boiling water, and soak for 20 minutes. Drain well, then chop the porcini into small pieces.

6. When the chicken is done, remove it from the baking dish, along with the onions, to a large bowl. Cover with foil to keep warm.

7. Scrape all the juices and drippings from the baking dish into a medium saucepan. Stir in the porcini, then cook briskly over high heat until the liquid has reduced to ¼ cup, about 20 minutes. As the sauce cooks, whisk in the remaining 4 tablespoons butter a little at a time until smooth. Remove from the heat and whisk in the salt and pepper. To serve, divide the polenta among the serving plates, then top with the chicken and onions. Drizzle with sauce and garnish with Parmigiano-Reggiano.

ITALIAN BEEF STEW SPEZZATINO DI MANZO

6 to 8 servings

ELVIRA PANTALEO ✳ This is the dish that inspired my husband to propose marriage.

2 pounds boneless **beef bottom round**, cut into 1½-inch cubes
½ teaspoon **salt**
½ teaspoon freshly ground **black pepper**
4 tablespoons **olive oil**
2 medium **onions**, chopped (about 2 cups)
2 medium **carrots**, chopped (about 1 cup)

4 medium yellow **potatoes** (about 1½ pounds), cut into 1½-inch cubes
2 cups dry **white wine**
2 cups **beef broth**, plus more as needed
1 cup **cherry tomatoes**, finely chopped
1½ cups shelled fresh **peas** or thawed frozen
¼ teaspoon **saffron**

1. Season the beef with the salt and pepper. Warm 2 tablespoons of the oil in a large pot or Dutch oven set over medium heat. Add half the beef and brown well, turning often, about 8 minutes. Transfer to a bowl, add the remaining 2 tablespoons oil, and brown the remainder of the beef, then transfer to the bowl.

2. Add the onions and carrots to the pot; cook, stirring often, until the onions begin to brown, about 10 minutes. Stir in the potatoes and cook, stirring occasionally, for 5 minutes.

3. Pour in the wine and scrape up any browned bits from the bottom of the pot. Raise the heat to medium-high and cook, stirring occasionally, until the wine has reduced to ¼ cup, about 12 minutes.

4. Pour in the broth, stir in the tomatoes, and return the beef and any juices that have collected in the bowl to the pot. Cover, reduce the heat, and simmer for 1 hour.

5. Stir in the peas and saffron. If the liquid in the pot is less than halfway up the beef pieces, add more broth to bring it to the correct level. Cover and cook until the beef is fork-tender, 30 to 40 minutes. Serve in bowls.

TRIPE with TOMATOES and WHITE WINE

TRIPPA CON POMODORI E VINO BIANCO

 4 servings

ADELINA ORAZZO ✳ This is the classic preparation of a beloved dish. The recipe doesn't make large servings because the meat is so rich.

1 pound cleaned **beef tripe**, cut into 2-inch pieces
2 tablespoons fresh **lemon juice**
2 **bay leaves**
2 tablespoons **olive oil**
¼ teaspoon **red pepper flakes**
1 small **onion**, diced (about ½ cup)

1 medium **carrot**, diced (about ½ cup)
2 medium **celery** stalks, thinly sliced (about 1 cup)
1 cup dry **white wine**
1 (14-ounce) can crushed **tomatoes**
¼ teaspoon **salt**
¼ teaspoon freshly ground **black pepper**

1. Place the tripe, lemon juice, and bay leaves in a large saucepan. Fill about three-quarters full with cool water and bring to a boil. Cook for 10 minutes. Drain. Discard the bay leaves.

2. Warm the oil in a large saucepan set over medium heat. Add the red pepper flakes; cook until aromatic, about 10 seconds. Add the onion, carrot, and celery; cook, stirring often, until the onion is lightly browned, about 5 minutes.

3. Pour in the wine and raise the heat to medium-high. Stir well to scrape any browned bits from the bottom of the pan and cook, stirring occasionally, until the liquid has reduced by half, about 5 minutes.

4. Stir in the tomatoes, salt, and black pepper, as well as the parboiled tripe. Return to a boil. Cover, reduce the heat, and simmer until the tripe is tender, about 35 minutes. Serve in bowls.

MEATBALLS WITH HARD-BOILED EGGS INSIDE

POLPETTE CON UOVA

6 servings

ADELINA ORAZZO ✳ I created my version of this classic dish to thank my neighbors for sharing a pig with my family. It was so dramatic that they asked, "Where do you get these ideas?" These meatballs taste as good as they look.

1 cup fresh **breadcrumbs**
2 tablespoons **olive oil**, plus more for the baking sheet
½ cup minced **onion**
1 teaspoon minced **garlic**
⅓ pound lean **ground beef**
⅓ pound **ground pork**
⅓ pound **ground veal**
2 large **eggs**, lightly beaten
1 ounce **Pecorino Romano**, finely grated (about ¼ cup)

2 tablespoons minced fresh **flat-leaf parsley**
½ teaspoon **salt**
½ teaspoon freshly ground **black pepper**, plus more for serving
6 hard-boiled **eggs**, peeled
Green salad tossed with a light vinaigrette, for serving (optional)

1. Soak the breadcrumbs in a small bowl with 1 cup water for 10 minutes. Squeeze them dry over the sink in small handfuls; transfer to a large bowl.

2. Warm the oil in a small skillet set over medium heat. Add the onion and garlic. Cook, stirring often, until softened, about 5 minutes. Scrape the onion and garlic into the bowl with the breadcrumbs and let cool for 10 minutes.

3. Position a rack in the center of the oven and preheat the oven to 350°F. Lightly oil a large rimmed baking sheet.

4. Crumble in the ground beef, pork, and veal and break them apart with a fork. Stir in the eggs, Pecorino Romano, parsley, salt, and pepper. Mix with clean hands until you have a uniform mixture.

5. Divide this meat mixture into six equal portions. Cup a portion in your palms, flatten and form the meat mixture to make a concave depression at its center; set a hard-boiled egg in this, then wrap and form the meat mixture into a ball around the egg, sealing it well on all sides with no gaps. Set on the baking sheet and repeat with the remainder of the meat mixture and eggs.

6. Bake until the meatballs are cooked through and browned, about 20 minutes. Serve with a tossed green salad, if desired.

MEAT LOAF WITH PARSLEY SAUCE

POLPETTONE CON SALSA VERDE

6 servings

CHRISTINA NARISI CARROZZA ✳ My family always makes meat loaf in the summer, to be served cold or at room temperature. Since it's made on the stovetop and not in the oven, it doesn't heat up the house. This recipe is a favorite with kids because the procedure is theatrical—tying up the meat in cheesecloth and lowering it into boiling water. It's as much fun to watch as the results are good to eat.

2 pounds lean **ground beef**
1½ cups fresh **breadcrumbs**
3 ounces **Parmigiano-Reggiano**, finely grated (about ¾ cup)
2 large **eggs**, lightly beaten
2 tablespoons minced fresh **flat-leaf parsley**

1 teaspoon plus 1 tablespoon **salt**
1 tablespoon minced **garlic**
½ teaspoon freshly ground **black pepper**
Salsa verde (page 213), for serving

1. Mix the ground beef, breadcrumbs, Parmigiano-Reggiano, eggs, parsley, 1 teaspoon salt, the garlic, and pepper in a large bowl with your hands until uniform. Shape the mixture into a 10-inch-long log. Stack two 12-inch squares of cheesecloth on your work surface, set the meat loaf on top, and roll the cheesecloth closed, tucking in and securing the sides (no open ends). Secure with butcher's twine in three or four places to hold the package closed.

2. Fill a large pot with water, add the remaining 1 tablespoon salt, and bring to a boil. Submerge the wrapped meat loaf, cover, reduce the heat, and simmer until an instant-read thermometer inserted into the center of the meat loaf registers 165°F, about 30 minutes.

3. Transfer the meat loaf to a cutting board. Cool the meat loaf for 10 minutes, then snip off the twine and remove the cheesecloth. Cut the meat loaf into ½-inch-thick rounds and serve with salsa verde drizzled over the top.

ROASTED VEAL LOIN ARROSTO DI VITELLO

 ── *6 servings* ├────┤

ROSA TURANO ✳ My mother didn't have an oven, so she did her roasting on the stove. I've maintained the tradition. You can find veal broth in the form of demi-glace in gourmet markets, but beef broth is fine. To accompany this dish, I roast baby potatoes my mother's way: in a covered pan over low heat with olive oil, butter, and sage, shaking them now and then, for 20 minutes or longer, until they're soft and lightly browned.

1 cup **all-purpose flour**, for dredging
1 (3½-pound) boneless **veal loin roast**
½ teaspoon **salt**
½ teaspoon freshly ground **black pepper**
3 tablespoons **butter**
4 tablespoons **olive oil**

2 large **onions**, halved and cut into thin half-moons
1 cup dry **white wine**
2 tablespoons minced fresh **sage**
1 cup **veal** or **beef broth**

1. Spread the flour on a large plate. Season the veal loin with the salt and pepper. Roll the veal in the flour, coating evenly on all sides. Shake off the excess flour.

2. Melt the butter in the oil in a large pot or Dutch oven set over medium-high heat. Add the veal and brown well, turning often, about 10 minutes. Transfer the veal to a cutting board.

3. Add the onions to the pot and cook, stirring often, until softened, about 8 minutes. Pour in the wine and scrape up any browned bits from the bottom of the pot. Stir in the sage. Return the veal to the pot, cover, reduce the heat, and simmer for 30 minutes.

4. Pour in the broth and return to a simmer. Cover and cook until the veal is tender, 30 to 45 minutes more.

5. Transfer the veal to a cutting board; let stand for 10 minutes. Cut into ¼-inch-thick rounds and serve in bowls with plenty of the onions and sauce ladled around the slices.

CALF'S LIVER in SWEET-AND-SOUR SAUCE

FEGATO DI VITELLO ALL'AGRODOLCE

 6 servings

MARGHERITA AMATO ✳ The *agrodolce*, or "sour" (*agro*) and "sweet" (*dolce*), elements in this sauce give calf's liver a more delicate flavor. Look for thin cutlets of liver or ask the butcher to slice them thin for you.

2 cups **all-purpose flour**, for dredging
2 pounds **calf's liver**, cut into ¼-inch-thick cutlets
8 tablespoons **olive oil**
2 large **onions**, halved and cut into thin half-moons

½ cup pitted **green olives**, halved
¼ cup **nonpareil capers** in brine, drained
1 tablespoon **sugar**
½ cup **white wine vinegar**
½ teaspoon **salt**
½ teaspoon freshly ground **black pepper**

1. Spread the flour on a large plate. Dredge the liver cutlets in the flour, coating both sides evenly and shaking off any excess. Transfer to a large cutting board.

2. Warm 2 tablespoons of the oil in a large skillet over medium-high heat. Slip in about one-third of the liver cutlets and cook, turning once, until medium-rare but well browned, about 6 minutes. Transfer to a serving platter. Cook the remainder of the liver cutlets in two more batches, adding 2 tablespoons oil before each batch.

3. Add the remaining 2 tablespoons oil to the skillet, then add the onions. Reduce the heat to medium and cook, stirring continuously, until lightly browned, about 10 minutes. Stir in the olives, capers, and sugar; cook for 1 minute, just until the sugar begins to caramelize.

4. Stir in the vinegar, salt, and pepper. Raise the heat to medium-high; cook until the liquid in the skillet has reduced by half, about 5 minutes. Spoon the sauce over the liver to serve.

COTECHINO AND LENTILS COTECHINO CON LENTICCHIE

6 servings

ROSA TURANO ✳ *Cotechino* is a special kind of pork sausage available in Italian markets and many butcher shops. My favorite lentils are the tiny ones: Italian castelluccio or Spanish pardina, which hold their shape during cooking. This dish is often served on New Year's Eve to bring luck in the year ahead.

2 **cotechino** (about 14 ounces each)
3 tablespoons unsalted **butter**
3 tablespoons **olive oil**
1 medium **onion**, chopped (about 1 cup)
2 medium **carrots**, chopped (about 1 cup)

2 medium **celery** stalks, thinly sliced (about 1 cup)
1 tablespoon minced **garlic**
2 cups brown **lentils**, rinsed
½ cup **tomato paste**
4½ cups **beef broth**

1. Place the cotechino in a large pot, add cold water to a depth of 2 inches above the cotechino, and bring to a boil. Cover, reduce the heat to low, and simmer until tender, about 2 hours.

2. Meanwhile, melt the butter in the oil in a large saucepan set over medium heat. Add the onion, carrots, celery, and garlic. Cook, stirring often, until the onion softens, about 7 minutes. Add the lentils and stir well. Stir in the tomato paste until it coats every lentil. Pour in the broth; then cover, reduce the heat, and simmer until the lentils are tender, about 30 minutes. Turn off the heat and set aside, covered, to keep warm as the cotechino cooks.

3. Transfer the cotechino to a large cutting board; let cool for 10 minutes. Remove the casings from the cotechino and cut the meat into 1-inch-thick rounds. Spoon and spread the lentil mixture onto a platter; top with the cotechino.

ROASTED PORK LOIN WITH ORANGES

LONZA DI MAIALE ARROSTO CON ARANCE

6 to 8 servings

CHRISTINA NARISI CARROZZA ✳ Lard is a common northern Italian ingredient, which I think of as an alternative to pancetta. You don't want the kind of lard that comes in a brick, which is pre-rendered, but sheets of fresh lard, available from the butcher. A roast with lard and oranges was one of my aunt Gianna's signature Sunday dishes.

3½ pounds boneless **pork loin**
½ teaspoon **salt**
½ teaspoon freshly ground **black pepper**
4 large thin **lard** slices (about 2 ounces)
3 (8-inch) fresh **rosemary** sprigs
5 tablespoons **olive oil**
¼ cup **orange liqueur**
¾ cup fresh **orange juice** (from 3 or 4 oranges)

1 cup dry **white wine**
¼ cup **juniper berries**
3 **bay leaves**
1 large **orange**, cut into ¼-inch-thick rounds and seeded
1 cup **chicken broth**, plus more as needed
3 tablespoons unsalted **butter**
3 tablespoons **all-purpose flour**

1. Season the pork loin with the salt and pepper. Lay the sheets of lard along the length of the pork on all sides. Wrap butcher's twine around the center of the pork and tie it securely to hold the lard in place. Slip a rosemary sprig lengthwise under the twine on three sides of the pork; secure in at least two more places (one on either end) with butcher's twine, holding the lard and rosemary against the pork.

2. Warm the oil in a large stock pot or Dutch oven set over medium-high heat. Add the pork and brown well on all sides, turning as needed, about 12 minutes. Transfer the pork to a cutting board.

3. Position the rack in the center of the oven and preheat the oven to 350°F.

4. Pour the fat out of the pot and return the pot to the heat. Add the liqueur. If it ignites, cover the pot and set aside for a couple of minutes before continuing with the recipe. Bring to a simmer and cook until reduced to a thick glaze, about 2 minutes. Add the orange juice, scrape any browned bits off the bottom of the pot, and cook until reduced to a thick glaze, about 5 minutes.

5. Add the wine, juniper berries, and bay leaves; return the pork to the pot. Bring to a simmer and cook until the wine has reduced by half, about 5 minutes.

6. Place the orange slices in an overlapping row on top of the pork; pour the broth around the pork. Bring to a simmer, cover, and place in the oven. Bake until an instant-read thermometer inserted into the pork registers 145°F, about 50 minutes. As the pork cooks, check the pot from time to time to make sure it's not dry and add more broth as needed. Turn the pork several times, first removing the orange slices and then putting them back on the new "top" after you've turned the pork.

7. Transfer the pork and orange slices to a carving board. Set aside for 10 minutes. Meanwhile, strain the liquid in the pot through a fine-mesh sieve into a small bowl. There should be at least ½ cup (add more broth if it's short). Melt the butter in a small saucepan over medium-low heat. Whisk in the flour until a paste forms. Whisk in the warm pan juices in a slow, steady stream until smooth. Continue whisking until thickened and bubbling, about 2 minutes.

8. Snip and remove the twine from the pork. Cut the pork it into ½-inch-thick rounds. Serve with the roasted orange slices and some of the thickened pan gravy.

ESCAPED BIRDS (OR PORK ROLLS WITH PANCETTA AND SAUSAGE) UCCELLI SCAPPATI

6 to 7 servings

CHRISTINA NARISI CARROZZA ✳ This recipe, created by my aunt Gianna in Italy, is delicious over polenta. It's become my family's customary New Year's Eve dinner because we like it better than cotechino.

12 (2-ounce) **pork cutlets**
½ teaspoon freshly ground **black pepper**
24 paper-thin slices **pancetta**
8 ounces mild **Italian sausage**, casings removed
12 large fresh **sage** leaves

4 tablespoons (½ stick) unsalted **butter**
½ cup dry **white wine**
2 (4-inch) fresh **rosemary** sprigs, plus mores for garnish
Classic Polenta (page 81), for serving

1. Lay a sheet of plastic wrap on a clean work surface, top with one cutlet, and lay a second sheet of plastic wrap over the meat. Pound to ¼ inch thick using the smooth side of a meat mallet or the bottom of a heavy saucepan. Peel off the top sheet of plastic wrap, set the cutlet aside, and repeat with the remainder of the cutlets, changing the plastic wrap as necessary. Season the cutlets with the pepper.

2. Top each cutlet with 2 slices pancetta, 1½ tablespoons sausage meat, and 1 sage leaf. Roll tightly and secure with a toothpick.

3. Melt the butter in a large skillet set over medium heat. Add the pork rolls and brown on all sides, turning often, about 10 minutes. Pour in the wine and add the rosemary sprigs. Return to a boil; then cover, reduce the heat, and simmer until tender, about 20 minutes.

4. To serve, discard the rosemary sprigs. Transfer the pork rolls to a carving board and slice into 1-inch pieces. Serve over polenta on individual plates with the pan juices poured over the top. Garnish with additional rosemary.

BOLLITO WITH PARSLEY SAUCE

BOLLITO MISTO CON SALSA VERDE

 10 to 12 servings

CHRISTINA NARISI CARROZZA ※ Bollito is a classic northern Italian stew, which might incorporate any inexpensive cut of meat, including tongue, or even turkey or capon. The name reflects the fact that all the ingredients are boiled together until tender. The typical accompaniment is Italian salsa verde made with parsley and anchovies, but Rosa Turano's husband is especially partial to Gorgonzola sauce.

FOR THE BOLLITO MISTO

1 tablespoon **salt**
2 teaspoons freshly ground **black pepper**
2 pounds boneless **pork butt**
2 pounds boneless **beef chuck**
2 pounds boneless **veal shoulder**

1 **cotechino** (about 1 pound)
6 large **carrots**, cut into 2-inch pieces
6 medium **celery** stalks, cut into 2-inch pieces
2 large **onions**, quartered

FOR THE SALSA VERDE

4 cups loosely packed fresh **flat-leaf parsley**
½ cup fresh **breadcrumbs**
¼ cup **nonpareil capers** in brine, drained

6 canned **anchovy fillets**
2 **garlic** cloves, sliced
3 tablespoons fresh **lemon juice**
1¼ cups extra-virgin **olive oil**

1. To make the bollito misto, fill a large stockpot or soup pot halfway with water; add the salt and pepper. Add the pork, beef, veal, cotechino, carrots, celery, and onions. Add more water to cover by at least 1 inch. Bring to a boil; cover, reduce the heat, and simmer until the meat is tender, 2 to 3 hours, adding more water as needed to make sure everything stays submerged.

2. Meanwhile, to make the salsa verde, place the parsley, breadcrumbs, capers, anchovies, garlic, and lemon juice in a food processor fitted with the chopping blade. Pulse until coarsely combined. Scrape down the inside of the canister, then continue pulsing while drizzling the oil through the feed tube until a coarse, loose sauce forms. The salsa verde can be made up to 2 days in advance and stored in the refrigerator sealed with plastic wrap touching the surface. Set on the counter for 20 minutes before using.

3. Transfer the cooked pork, beef, veal, and cotechino to a large cutting board. Transfer the carrots and celery to a serving platter. Discard the onions and the water in the pot. Remove the casing from the cotechino and slice it and all the other meats into 1-inch pieces. Place on the platter with the vegetables. Dollop with some of the salsa verde, serving the remainder on the side.

VARIATION

GORGONZOLA SAUCE SALSA DI GORGONZOLA

about 2¼ cups

ROSA TURANO

2 cups regular **mayonnaise**
5 ounces **Gorgonzola** (about 1¼ cups)
2 tablespoons **Dijon mustard**

¼ teaspoon **salt**
¼ teaspoon freshly ground **black pepper**

Place the mayonnaise, Gorgonzola, mustard, salt, and pepper in a food processor fitted with the chopping blade. Process until smooth, scraping down the inside of the canister at least once. Serve with meat and vegetables, or on the side if you're also serving the salsa verde.

LAMB STEW with CREAMY CHEESE SAUCE

STUFATO DI AGNELLO CON CREMA DI FORMAGGIO E UOVA

 6 servings

ROSARIA VIGORITO ✳ My mother's region of Italy, Abruzzo, is famous for its lamb. Some people substitute veal in this classic dish, but lamb is traditional—and delicious.

6 tablespoons **olive oil**

2 pounds boneless **leg of lamb**, trimmed and cut into 1-inch cubes

1 large **onion**, halved and cut into thin half-moons

1 cup dry **white wine**

½ teaspoon **salt**

½ teaspoon freshly ground **black pepper**

1½ cups **chicken broth**

4 large **eggs**, at room temperature

4 ounces **Pecorino Romano**, finely grated (about 1 cup)

1. Warm 2 tablespoons of the oil in a large pot or Dutch oven set over medium heat. Add half the lamb and brown it well, turning often, about 6 minutes. Transfer to a large bowl, add 2 tablespoons more oil, and brown the remainder of the lamb, then transfer to the bowl.

2. Add the remaining 2 tablespoons oil to the pot, then add the onion. Cook, stirring often, until the onion has wilted, about 4 minutes. Pour in the wine and scrape up any browned bits from the bottom of the pot. Raise the heat to medium-high and cook until the wine has reduced by half, about 10 minutes.

3. Return the lamb to the pot; stir in the salt and pepper as well as ¼ cup of the broth. Cover, reduce the heat to very low, and simmer until the lamb is tender, about 1½ hours, stirring in ¼ cup more broth every 15 minutes. Transfer the lamb to a deep serving dish. Remove the pot from the heat.

4. In a second bowl, whisk the eggs and Pecorino Romano until well blended. Whisk 1 cup of the pan sauce in a slow, steady stream into this mixture until smooth, then whisk the combined mixture into the remaining sauce in the pot. Set the pot over the lowest heat possible and whisk continuously until creamy and smooth, not even 1 minute. Do not boil or the eggs will curdle. Pour the sauce over the lamb before serving.

RACK OF LAMB WITH TOMATOES AND POTATOES

CARRÉ DI AGNELLO CON POMODORI E PATATE

 4 servings

ROSARIA VIGORITO ✳ This is my family's favorite way to roast lamb: with potatoes and lots of garlic. The same ingredients are delicious with rabbit.

1½ pounds medium **Yukon Gold potatoes**, quartered
4 tablespoons **olive oil**
1 tablespoon minced **garlic**
1 teaspoon **salt**

½ teaspoon freshly ground **black pepper**
1 (8-bone, 1½-pound) **rack of lamb**, trimmed and frenched (see note)
1 (28-ounce) can crushed **tomatoes**
Torn fresh **flat-leaf parsley**, for garnish

1. Position the rack in the center of the oven and preheat the oven to 350°F.

2. Toss the potatoes with 2 tablespoons of the oil, the garlic, ½ teaspoon of the salt, and ¼ teaspoon of the pepper in a large roasting pan. Roast, tossing occasionally, for 20 minutes.

3. Nestle the rack of lamb, bone side down, into the potatoes. Pour the tomatoes over and around the meat. Drizzle the meat with the remaining 2 tablespoons oil; sprinkle with the remaining ½ teaspoon salt and ¼ teaspoon pepper.

4. Roast until an instant-read thermometer inserted into the eye of meat without touching the bone registers 125°F for rare or 135°F for medium. Transfer the rack of lamb to a carving board or serving platter, arrange the potatoes around the meat, and set aside for 10 minutes before carving between the bones. Sprinkle with parsley to serve.

◁ **NOTE** ▷ *A frenched rack of lamb has all the meat, fat, and cartilage removed between the bones for a more elegant presentation. To french, slice between the rib bones down the long tube of meat (the "eye") that lies at one end of the bones; scrape off all the bits on the bones, cleaning them completely. Many butcher shops and high-end markets sell already frenched racks of lamb.*

BAKED LAMB'S HEAD CAPUZZELLE DI AGNELLO

6 servings

NINA PICARIELLO ✳ When I was growing up in the mountains near Salerno, neighbors would gather to roast a whole lamb, and my grandmother always claimed the head, or *capuzzelle.*

1 **lamb's head** (2½ to 3 pounds), split
1 cup dry **white wine**
4 tablespoons **olive oil**
1 medium **lemon**, cut into thin rings and seeded
3 **garlic** cloves, coarsely chopped

½ teaspoon **salt**
½ teaspoon freshly ground **black pepper**
Freshly grated **Parmigiano-Reggiano**, for garnish
Minced fresh **flat-leaf parsley**, for garnish

1. Set both lamb's head halves in a very large pot, pour in the wine, and add enough water so the meat is submerged by 2 inches. Bring to a boil. Reduce the heat to medium-low and simmer for 20 minutes. Transfer the lamb's head halves to a cutting board and let cool for 15 minutes.

2. Position the rack in the center of the oven and preheat the oven to 350°F.

3. Overlap and seal two 20-inch sheets of aluminum foil on your work surface to form a single piece; top with two overlapping sheets of parchment paper. Set half the lamb's head in the center; drizzle with half the oil and scatter half the lemon slices, half the garlic, half the salt, and half the pepper over the meat. Fold the packet closed and seal very tightly. Transfer to a large rimmed baking sheet or a roasting pan and repeat with the other lamb's head half in a second packet.

4. Bake for 1 hour 10 minutes, until the meat on the bones is very tender. Let cool on a wire rack for 10 minutes, then open the packets and cool for 10 minutes more. Transfer the lamb's head halves to a serving platter and garnish with Parmigiano-Reggiano and parsley. To serve, use a serving fork to pull the meat off the bones; peel the exterior skin off the tongue before carving it into small rounds.

MY NONNA'S RABBIT

CONIGLIO DI MIA NONNA

 4 servings

ROSA TURANO ✳ I still make this dish exactly as my nonna did, including her secret ingredient—cinnamon. I like to serve it over polenta.

1 (4-pound) **rabbit**, cut into 8 pieces, liver and kidneys chopped and reserved
½ teaspoon **salt**
½ teaspoon freshly ground **black pepper**
4 tablespoons **olive oil**
1 cup dry **white wine**
1 (28-ounce) can diced **tomatoes**
1 medium **onion**, chopped (about 1 cup)

1 medium **carrot**, diced (about ½ cup)
2 medium **celery** stalks, thinly sliced (about 1 cup)
1 tablespoon minced **garlic**
10 fresh **sage** leaves, chopped
2 (4-inch) fresh **rosemary** sprigs
1 **cinnamon** stick
Classic Polenta (page 81), for serving

1. Season the rabbit with the salt and pepper. Warm 2 tablespoons of the oil in a large pot or Dutch oven set over medium heat. Add the rabbit and brown well, turning once, about 7 minutes.

2. Pour in the wine and bring to a boil. Cook until the wine has been reduced to a thick glaze, about 10 minutes. Transfer the rabbit to a large bowl.

3. Add the remaining 2 tablespoons oil, then stir in the tomatoes, onion, carrot, celery, garlic, sage, rosemary, and cinnamon stick, as well as the liver and kidneys. Cook, uncovered and stirring occasionally, for 10 minutes.

4. Return the rabbit with any juices that have collected in the bowl to the pot. Cover, lower the heat, and simmer until the rabbit is fork-tender, about 1 hour. Serve in bowls over polenta, with any pan juices drizzled over the top.

X

DOLCI

JODY SCARAVELLA *My Nonna Domenica, a phenomenal cook, was also an expert baker. I loved her lemon cookies, biscotti, and cakes, but my absolute favorite was a kind of peppery biscuit she made. So far, I haven't met a nonna who knows how to make that, but I keep hoping. In the meantime, there are so many other Italian sweets to enjoy, from classic fig cookies and ricotta pastries to blueberry or chocolate crostatas.*

Teresa Scalici

One night at the Enoteca, I heard that Jody was looking for me. "What the hell does he want?" I said. Because if he wants you, it's either all good or all bad.

So I left the downstairs kitchen for the restaurant, where I saw

our state legislator from Staten Island eating at the bar. She's a regular, and she loves me. Whenever I see her, we hug and kiss.

She was with Jody. "The legislator has a question," he said. "These Nutella cookies—are they different?"

My Nutella cookies are her favorite, and she buys extras. But I didn't want to lie. I said, "Madam, I've got to tell you the truth. I changed them."

They couldn't believe it. "Why?"

"Because this recipe is two hundred years old," I told them.

They thought that I meant "twenty years old," mistaking the English. So I got my purse to show them. Inside I had the recipe, in Italian, in my nonna's handwriting. "This is the way my nonna, and her mother, made these cookies," I said. "With figs, chocolate, and anisette or rum, instead of Nutella, *pignoli,* and walnuts."

Well, they were amazed. The legislator said, "These cookies are the best!"

People clap their hands when I make food the way my nonna Rosalia taught me. I always knew she deserved to go to heaven. But when people go crazy for her recipes, I think, "Now I know she made it. She's really up there, happy."

I'm the youngest of five children, four girls and one boy. People think the baby of the family always gets spoiled, but that wasn't true for me. Every time I needed a dress, they'd take an old one off my sister, turn the material, and make me wear it. I used to cry to my mother, "You don't like me. I'm the leftover."

I also felt overworked. My oldest sisters, Concetta and Rosalia, had married. Being a boy, my brother, Vincenzo, got off easy. So my sister Vita and I were stuck with the chores. "How come we do it all?" Vita asked. "It's so hard. You don't even help." My mother said, "You buy a fork so you don't have to eat with your hands."

"What does she mean?" I asked Vita, who was two years older. She explained: To my mother, we were forks.

So I got the idea that I'd have a better life with Nonna Rosalia. She was a widow, having lost my grandfather during World War II, before I was born. Since she lived two blocks away, I'd go to the same school and keep the same friends. But she'd give me her full attention and, I was sure, would baby me.

I was ten when I went to live with her. After school, I wanted to play outside with my friends. "Why?" my nonna asked. "Don't you want to get married? When your husband gets home, he'll want to see food on the table."

What? I didn't expect my loving nonna to put me to work. But she did, every day, teaching me to cook. I started with gnocchi because it's the simplest. We made ours with ricotta, flour, and eggs—never with potatoes. Ricotta gnocchi are very light, and you can add anything you want, like spinach. My nonna sat right next to me while I mixed the dough with my hands, so I would get the feel. She cooked by touch, not by measuring. I noticed the little scale in her kitchen and asked what it was for, since she never used it. When she told me, I said, "Nonna, if we weigh the flour and ricotta, you won't have to watch me. I can make gnocchi by myself."

She seemed surprised but said we could try it. So when she taught me to make pasta—pappardelle, tagliatelle—we weighed the flour, then added salt and eggs. Then I'd have to roll out the dough, which was hard, trying to grip the rolling pin with my little hands. My nonna didn't care. "Thinner," she'd say. "No good."

When my sheet of pasta was thin enough, we'd let it lie on the wooden tabletop, covered with a blanket, to dry for at least an hour. When it felt right, my nonna had me cut it by folding it into layers, then slicing crosswise through the layers to make strands—wide for pappardelle, narrower for tagliatelle. But she was strict: my cuts had to be perfect, so when I lifted each noodle with a knife tip to shake out the folds, the strands all looked the same.

I got so frustrated. Sometimes I'd cry, "I don't want to make pasta today." But when I finally cut a batch of perfect tagliatelle, my nonna was so thrilled that she bought me a gift.

Today, because it's easier, most people cut pasta dough with a machine. But thanks to my nonna, I still cut my pasta the way she taught me, with a knife. And I cook it her way, too: boil water in a pot; add two spoonfuls of oil and then the pasta; stir only once. When the pasta rises to the surface, it's ready.

Though I was living with my nonna, I had family responsibilities. We had a farm in Cammarata in Agrigento, an agricultural province on the southern coast of Sicily.

My father and his brother kept a small herd of
cows. Their milk, the cheese we made from it,
and various cash crops supported our family. My
mother worked alongside my father on the farm,
and so did we.

It seemed that every month in the fall, there
was something new to harvest: oranges, lemons,
almonds, olives. The almonds we gathered in
August were two inches long, with a fuzzy, thick
skin and an inner shell to crack to reach the part
you eat, the seed. November was the month for

My mother and my son, 1969

olives. We'd cover the ground with blankets, then my father would beat the olive tree
branches with a stick and knock the fruit to the ground for Vita and me to gather, on
our knees.

But our little farm was failing. When our cows died, my mother cried as if we were
losing loved ones. Luckily, my father was well respected, so a rich landowner hired
him to manage a farm in Torretta, closer to Palermo. Laborers did the farmwork there,
so for me and Vita, the chief responsibilities changed to household chores and, more
important, completing our trousseaus.

Like most Italian girls, I'd begun needlework training around the age of twelve. In
Torretta, we found a woman who sold embroidery patterns. Every penny I scrounged
went to gorgeous colored thread and new designs—angels kissing each other, beautiful
leafy trees—to embroider on the sheets I was collecting for my marriage.

I met Calogero, who became my husband, in Torretta. He was so handsome—
then and now—and by the time I was sixteen, I had a ring. Soon afterward, he and his
family left Sicily, in search of work, and settled in Manhattan's Hell's Kitchen. When
construction jobs dried up, my brother, Vincenzo, left too, for Bayonne, New Jersey.
Vincenzo walked me down the aisle, at a beautiful church in Bayonne, when I was
nineteen.

I began life as a bride in a rented apartment in Bensonhurst, Brooklyn. All I had in
my kitchen were two skillets, two pots, six plates; six each of knives, forks, and spoons;
and six drinking glasses, which did double duty for water and wine. You'd think those
glasses were made of the finest crystal, if you saw how gingerly I washed and dried them.

Calogero did carpentry, and I got a job in a garment factory. The owner was so amazed that I could work five machines that she paid me an extra $30 a week. Today that would be more than $200. Everyone in those factories—bosses and workers—was Italian. At home, we'd all speak in our own dialects; and in Bensonhurst, we spoke Italian. That was killing us. People lived here for twenty, thirty, or forty years without a word of English—not even knowing how to say "yes." We were that isolated.

Luckily, I learned to speak English once I had kids. Within a few years of my marriage, I had one, two, three, right in a row: Raffaele, Giuseppe, and Giuseppina.

With three children, we needed more space, but found few landlords willing to tolerate a noisy young family. So we bought a lot on Staten Island, and Calogero fulfilled his dream of building us a house, using his master-carpenter/contractor skills, to the same exacting standards that he guaranteed for his high-end clients.

The most important part—the heart—of our house is the garden. From the beginning we planned to have our ground-floor apartment open to the outdoors. We have olive, persimmon, and fig trees, along with all kinds of herbs and vegetables. The garden is an extension of our living and eating space, where we can comfortably serve a meal for forty people. We had to wait a year, once the house was done, for the earth to settle so we could furnish the garden with a family-size table of hand-poured concrete, topped with beautiful ceramic tile.

Calogero also built a barbecue pit out there, with a roof, so we can grill in any weather, along with a garage-size space housing an inset wood-burning pizza oven. I knew that the oven was imported from Italy and had to be expensive. When I asked Calogero how much it cost, he said, "Maybe $2,000. But don't worry about it. I got it for nothing." Later, though, he told a friend, "You can imagine how hard I had to work to get something like that for free!"

My life with Calogero is a true partnership. He's always worked hard to keep bread on our table, and I've worked hard to manage our lives. It's a traditional relationship, and I love my role, especially the cooking and entertaining. Still, I know the world is changing. Once, my son got up to clear his dishes, and Calogero said, "Relax. Let the women do it." Well, my daughter got furious. She was a breadwinner herself, with a job in New York City. She said, "Why should I clean up after my brother?" When I was young, though we worked on the farm, we'd serve my brother his food and iron his pants when he went out. Back then, it was expected. But now, I

My Best Lasagna Prize, 2008

told Calogero, "She's right. It's not fair."

He shrugged and said, "Men are men." He's old-fashioned.

But for him, old-fashioned means that his focus, like mine, is always on the family's needs. That's the way we've built our life together—as a team—for close to fifty years.

When I was sixty, I got restless. My kids were grown and my household ran like clockwork. I had so much energy left over, I thought I should get a job. I said so to my neighbor when we were out shoveling snow, wondering if I could get factory work.

"You've got to be kidding," he said. "I could sell anything you cooked."

I laughed. But the next morning, I pulled my coat over my pajamas and went out to get the papers. There was Jody's ad, looking for nonnas who made traditional dishes.

When I went to the Enoteca, they questioned me: "Can you make focaccia? How about caponata?" I thought, "What have I been eating all my life? Are you crazy?"

But what I said was, "Just try me out, and if I'm no good, you don't have to pay me."

Believe me, I got paid that night, and I've been cooking there ever since.

Working at the Enoteca has given me the chance to share a precious legacy. When my nonna died in the 1970s, she was almost a hundred years old. The next time I went to Italy, my mother pulled me aside to say, "Nonna left you something."

She handed me an antique box that held some earrings, eighteen-carat gold with milky blue stones. "They were her engagement gift from your nonno," my mother said. "She rarely wore them because she was scared she'd lose them."

So beautiful! Along with the earrings was a book. I always heard that as a child, learning to cook, my nonna had written down our family recipes. Of course, by the time I knew her, she didn't need them. She cooked by instinct, look, and feel. But it stayed in the family, and here it was—that legendary book—handed down to me.

What treasures. My sisters were all jealous, but I said, "I was the one stuck in the house, working with nonna." Wasn't that lucky?

FIG COOKIES CUCCIDATI

CHRISTINA NARISI CARROZZA ✳ *Cuccidati*, also called *buccellati*, are a beloved Italian treat. Elvira Pantaleo's family used to eat them on December 8, the Feast of the Immaculate Conception. Teresa Scalici makes a version, *biscotti collafico*, from her nonna's centuries-old recipe. Margherita Amato's family has a traditional multigenerational Christmas buccellati contest. My family has a similar holiday custom, everyone gathering to make cuccidati from this recipe handed down by my nonna.

FOR THE FILLING
1½ cups **chocolate chips**, preferably
  bittersweet
1 cup blanched **almonds**
1 cup **walnut** pieces
1 cup diced **citron**
½ cup **maple syrup**, preferably grade B

6 dried **figs**, stemmed and quartered
8 large pitted **dates**, halved
1 tablespoon ground **cinnamon**
1 tablespoon finely grated **orange zest**
1 teaspoon **vanilla extract**

FOR THE DOUGH
5½ cups **all-purpose flour**, plus more
  for dusting
1 tablespoon **baking powder**
¼ teaspoon **salt**
1⅓ cups solid **vegetable shortening**

1½ cups **granulated sugar**
4 large **egg yolks**, at room temperature
1 tablespoon **vanilla extract**
1 cup plus 2 tablespoons whole or
  low-fat **milk**

FOR THE GLAZE
2 cups **confectioners' sugar**
3 tablespoons whole or low-fat **milk**,
  plus more as needed

1. To make the filling, put the chocolate chips, almonds, walnuts, citron, maple syrup, figs, dates, cinnamon, orange zest, and vanilla in a food processor fitted with the chopping blade. Process until a coarse paste forms, scraping down the inside of the canister at least once. Transfer to a medium bowl. The filling can be made 2 days in advance; cover and refrigerate but set on the counter to come to room temperature before using.

2. To make the dough, whisk the flour, baking powder, and salt in a large bowl. Put the shortening and granulated sugar in a second large bowl; beat with a handheld mixer on medium speed until creamy and thick, about 4 minutes, occasionally scraping down the

inside of the bowl with a rubber spatula. Beat in the egg yolks one at a time, then beat in the vanilla until smooth.

3. With the mixer on low speed, beat in half the flour until combined. Beat in half the milk until smooth, scrape down the bowl, and beat in the remainder of the flour just until moistened. Beat in the remainder of the milk until a soft dough forms, no more than 1 minute to make sure you don't overwork the glutens. Cover the bowl and refrigerate for at least 30 minutes or up to 1 day.

4. Divide the oven into thirds with two racks and preheat the oven to 375°F. Line two large rimmed baking sheets with parchment paper.

5. Divide the dough into 4 pieces. Dust a clean work surface with flour and set a piece of dough on top. (Refrigerate the remaining pieces until you're ready to use them.) Dust a rolling pin with flour and roll the dough into an 11 x 4-inch rectangle.

6. Spoon, spread, and form one-quarter of the filling into the middle of the dough; roll it into a log, starting with one long side. Pinch the ends together and set seam side down on your work surface. Cut the log into 1-inch-thick slices on a 45-degree angle. Place the cookies, spacing them 2 inches apart, on one of the baking sheets.

7. Repeat steps 5 and 6 with the other pieces of dough and the rest of the filling.

8. Bake in the top third and bottom third of the oven for 8 minutes. Reverse the baking sheets top to bottom and turn them back to front. Continue baking until lightly browned, about 7 minutes more.

9. Meanwhile, make the glaze. Whisk the confectioners' sugar and milk in a medium bowl until creamy and smooth. If it's too thick, whisk in a teaspoon or two of milk; if it's too thin, add more confectioners' sugar in 2 tablespoon increments.

10. Set a wire rack over paper towels on your work surface. Transfer the baking sheets to the rack to cool for 2 minutes. Place the cookies on the wire racks; brush the cookies while warm with the glaze (which will drip down onto the paper towels). Let cool to room temperature, about 2 hours. Store between sheets of parchment paper in a sealed container at room temperature for up to 3 days or in the freezer for up to 4 months.

HONEY-GLAZED DOUGH BALLS STRUFFOLI

6 to 8 servings

ADELINA ORAZZO ✳ *Struffoli*, tiny balls of deep-fried dough, are a famous Neapolitan treat.

FOR THE DOUGH BALLS
4 large **eggs**, at room temperature
¼ cup **sugar**
1 tablespoon unsalted **butter**, melted
 and cooled

1 tablespoon **brandy** or **rum**
2⅓ cups **all-purpose flour**, plus more
 as needed
Canola or **vegetable oil**, for frying

FOR THE GLAZE AND GARNISH
1 cup **honey**
½ cup moderately dry **white wine**
Chopped **glacéed (candied) fruit**, such
 as orange or lemon peel

Rainbow **nonpareils**, for garnish

1. To make the dough balls, whisk the eggs, sugar, butter, and brandy in a large bowl until smooth and creamy, about 3 minutes. Use a wooden spoon to stir in the flour until a soft dough forms, adding a little more flour if the dough is sticky. Cover and let rest for 10 minutes.

2. Divide the dough into 6 equal pieces; roll each piece of dough into a log about ½ inch in diameter. Cut the logs into ½-inch pieces.

3. Line a large baking sheet with paper towels. Pour 3 inches of oil into a large saucepan and clip a deep-frying thermometer to the inside of the pan. Heat the oil over medium heat until it registers 325°F. Add about one-quarter of the balls and fry until golden, turning often and adjusting the heat to keep the oil's temperature constant, about 2 minutes. Use a slotted spoon to transfer the fried balls to the baking sheet and continue frying in batches.

4. To make the glaze, bring the honey and wine to a boil in a large saucepan set over medium heat, stirring until the honey dissolves. Simmer until reduced to about two-thirds of its original volume, about 2 minutes. Remove from the heat, pour the balls into the glaze, and toss with two wooden spoons until coated. Let cool for 3 minutes.

5. Pour the balls onto a serving platter and form into a mound or sharp pyramid. Sprinkle with glacéed fruit and nonpareils.

CHOCOLATE BLOOD PUDDING SANGUINACCIO

 ———————————————————————————————— *6 servings* ⊢——⊣

FRANCESCA LEONE ✳ In Calabrian dialect, we call this pudding *sanguinazzu*. It's not a dish you'll find listed on restaurant menus, but if you ever come across it, be sure to try it. If you're curious about traditional foods, here's how to make it. You can get pig's blood at Italian or other good butcher shops.

1 teaspoon whole **cloves**
2 **cinnamon** sticks, broken into
   smaller pieces
2 wide **orange zest** strips
2 quarts **red wine**
½ cup **sugar**

4 cups **pig's blood**
7 ounces semisweet **chocolate**,
   melted and cooled
1 tablespoon ground **cinnamon**
1 tablespoon **honey**
1 cup **walnut** pieces, chopped

1. Place the cloves, cinnamon sticks, and orange zest in a tea ball. Alternatively, tie them into a cheesecloth sachet. Set the tea ball in a large saucepan; add the wine and sugar. Bring to a boil over medium-high heat, stirring until the sugar dissolves. Continue boiling for 40 minutes. Remove the tea ball and boil the liquid until reduced to a syrup, 30 to 45 minutes more. Let cool to room temperature, about 1 hour.

2. Pour the pig's blood into the top half of a double boiler. If you see any lumps, set the top of the double boiler over 1 inch of simmering water. Stir continuously just until warm. Immediately remove the top half of the double boiler from the heat.

3. Pour the blood through a fine-mesh sieve into a bowl, removing any lumps. Stir in the wine reduction, chocolate, and ground cinnamon.

4. Wipe out the top of the double boiler; pour the blood mixture into it. Set it back over the simmering water and stir just until warm. Stir in the honey. Continue stirring until the mixture resembles a pudding. Remove from the heat and stir in the walnuts. Let cool for 15 minutes, then pour into a bowl and refrigerate for up to 3 days before serving cold.

SICILIAN MILK PUDDING BIANCOMANGIARE

 6 servings

CHRISTINA NARISI CARROZZA ✳ In Italy, my nonna Christina would make us birthday cakes by layering ladyfingers or cookies with this kind of pudding.

4 cups whole **milk**
1 cup **sugar**
¼ cup **cornstarch**
¼ teaspoon **salt**

1 **cinnamon** stick
Shaved dark or bittersweet **chocolate**,
 for garnish

1. Whisk the milk, sugar, cornstarch, and salt in a large saucepan set over low heat until the sugar dissolves. Add the cinnamon stick and cook, stirring with a wooden spoon all the while, until thick and bubbling, about 7 minutes.

2. Remove and discard the cinnamon stick. Pour the mixture into six 1- to 1½-cup ramekins. Let cool for 10 minutes. Top with chocolate and serve warm.

VARIATION

To make a chocolate milk pudding, whisk 2 ounces finely chopped unsweetened chocolate into the saucepan with the milk and other ingredients. Cook as directed over low heat, stirring continuously, until the mixture thickens and the chocolate melts, about 8 minutes. Discard the cinnamon stick, divide the pudding among the ramekins, garnish with chopped candied ginger, and serve warm.

STUFFED BAKED PEACHES PESCHE AL FORNO RIPIENE

6 servings

CHRISTINA NARISI CARROZZA ✳ During peach season, the height of summer, this dessert is light and refreshing. Be sure to look for balsamic glaze, which is different from balsamic vinegar, in the supermarket.

6 large **peaches**, halved and pitted
½ cup packed **light brown sugar**
2 cups **mascarpone**

¾ cup **confectioners' sugar**
½ cup chopped roasted **almonds**
¼ cup **balsamic glaze**

1. Position the rack in the middle of the oven and preheat the oven to 375°F.

2. Arrange the peaches cut side up on a large rimmed baking sheet. Sprinkle evenly with the brown sugar. Bake until tender but not soft, and the sugar has melted and is bubbling, about 25 minutes. Transfer the baking sheet to a wire rack and let cool to room temperature, about 1 hour.

3. Place the mascarpone and confectioners' sugar in a food processor fitted with the chopping blade. Process until smooth. Scrape the mixture into a medium bowl and stir in the almonds.

4. Fill the centers of the peaches evenly with the mascarpone mixture, about 2 tablespoons per peach. Refrigerate for 1 hour. Drizzle each peach with 1 teaspoon balsamic glaze to serve.

FRIED RICOTTA TURNOVERS CASSATELLE DI RICOTTA

 18 turnovers

TERESA SCALICI ✳ These are my nonna's traditional Sicilian turnovers.

FOR THE DOUGH
3 cups **bread flour**
½ cup **canola oil**
½ cup dry **red wine**

2 large **egg yolks**, lightly beaten
1 tablespoon **granulated sugar**
1 teaspoon **vanilla extract**

FOR THE FILLING
3 cups whole-milk **ricotta**
¾ cup **granulated sugar**

½ teaspoon ground **cinnamon**
½ teaspoon **vanilla extract**

Canola or **vegetable oil**, for frying
Confectioners' sugar, for garnish

1. To make the dough, place the flour in a large bowl; add the oil, wine, egg yolks, granulated sugar, and vanilla. Stir with a wooden spoon until a soft dough forms. Cover and refrigerate for 1½ hours.

2. To make the filling, stir the ricotta, granulated sugar, cinnamon, and vanilla in a second bowl until the sugar dissolves.

3. Divide the dough into eighteen equal balls, about 2 tablespoons each. Roll one into a 5-inch circle; set 1½ tablespoons of the filling in the center. Fold closed to make a half-moon; crimp the edge with a fork to seal well. Set on a large rimmed baking sheet and make the remainder of the turnovers. Set the baking sheet in the freezer for 30 minutes.

4. Set a wire rack over paper towels. Pour 3 inches of oil into a large saucepan and clip a deep-frying thermometer to the inside of the pan. Heat the oil over medium heat until it registers 325°F. Add 6 turnovers and fry until golden and firm, turning once and adjusting the heat to keep the oil's temperature constant, about 4 minutes. Transfer to the wire rack to drain and continue frying the remainder of the turnovers in two more batches. Serve warm or at room temperature. Dust with confectioners' sugar.

SWEET MANICOTTI MANICOTTI DOLCI

6 to 8 servings (18 manicotti)

TERESA SCALICI ✳ I usually fill these crepes with sweetened ricotta, but feel free to experiment by adding or substituting anything you like. Other fillings I like to play with include marmalade, jam, and Nutella.

4 large **eggs**, at room temperature
1½ tablespoons plus ½ cup **sugar**
1 tablespoon **vegetable oil**
1 tablespoon **vanilla extract**
1 cup **all-purpose flour**
Cooking spray

3 cups whole-milk or low-fat **ricotta**
1 cup **blueberries**
1 cup sliced hulled **strawberries**
Store-bought **chocolate sauce**, for
  garnish

1. Whisk the eggs, 1½ tablespoons of the sugar, the oil, and vanilla with 1 cup water in a medium bowl until smooth. Whisk in the flour a little at a time, until you have a thin pancake batter.

2. Coat an 8-inch nonstick skillet with cooking spray and set over medium-low heat for a minute or two. Pour in 2 tablespoons of the batter; swirl the skillet to form an even, thin crepe. Cook for 1 minute, then use tongs to peel up and flip the crepe. Cook until golden, about 20 seconds. Transfer to a plate or cutting board and continue making more crepes, piling them one on top of another.

3. Stir the ricotta and the remaining ½ cup sugar in a second medium bowl until the sugar dissolves. Lay a crepe on a clean work surface; fill with 2 tablespoons of the sweetened ricotta and 2 tablespoons of either blueberries or strawberries (or a combination). Roll up, continue stuffing the remainder of the crepes, and drizzle with chocolate sauce to serve.

PUMPKIN CHEESECAKE TORTA DI ZUCCA E MASCARPONE

 8 servings

CHRISTINA NARISI CARROZZA ✳ The young adults with whom I managed a café helped develop this Italian-accented cheesecake.

FOR THE CRUST
1½ cups **amaretto cookie crumbs**
¼ cup **sugar**

5 tablespoons unsalted **butter**, melted and cooled, plus butter for the pan

FOR THE CAKE
8 ounces regular **cream cheese** (about 1 cup)
1 cup **mascarpone**
¾ cup **sugar**
2 large **eggs**, at room temperature

½ teaspoon **vanilla extract**
1 cup canned **pumpkin puree** (do not use pumpkin pie filling)
½ teaspoon ground **cinnamon**
⅛ teaspoon freshly grated **nutmeg**

Whipped cream, for serving

1. Position the rack in the center of the oven and preheat the oven to 375°F. Generously butter a 9-inch springform pan.

2. To make the crust, combine the cookie crumbs, sugar, and melted butter in a medium bowl until moistened. Pour into the cake pan and press to cover the bottom and go up the sides by 1 inch.

3. To make the cake, beat the cream cheese and mascarpone in a large bowl with a hand-held mixer at medium speed until smooth. Beat in the sugar until light and fluffy. Beat in the eggs one at a time, then the vanilla until smooth. Pour 1 cup batter onto the crust in the cake pan.

4. Beat the pumpkin, cinnamon, and nutmeg into the remaining batter until smooth. Pour and spread gently over the plain batter in the crust.

5. Bake until set with a slight jiggle at the center of the cake when tapped, 40 to 50 minutes. Transfer to a wire rack and let cool for 1 hour. Run a knife around the inside of the cake pan to loosen the cake. Continue to cool to room temperature, about another hour. Cover with plastic wrap and refrigerate for at least 24 hours or up to 3 days. Unlatch the springform ring and remove it. Cover the cake in whipped cream before slicing and serving.

BLUEBERRY TART CROSTATA DI MIRTILLI

 8 servings

ROSARIA VIGORITO ✳ This classic *crostata*, made with homemade blueberry jam, is my signature dessert at the Enoteca.

FOR THE BLUEBERRY JAM
1 pint **blueberries**
¼ cup **sugar**

FOR THE CRUST

2½ cups **all-purpose flour**, plus more for rolling
⅔ cup **sugar**
2 teaspoons finely grated **lemon zest**
1 teaspoon **salt**

12 tablespoons (1½ sticks) unsalted **butter**, diced and kept chilled in the refrigerator
1 large **egg** plus 2 large **egg yolks**, at room temperature, lightly beaten

Whipped cream, for garnish (optional)

1. To make the jam, heat the blueberries in a small saucepan set over medium heat until they begin to bubble, stirring frequently and smashing the berries against the inside of the pan, about 7 minutes. Stir in the sugar and bring to a boil. Cook, stirring continuously, until thickened, about 5 minutes. Remove from the heat to cool to room temperature, about 1 hour. The jam can be made up to 1 day in advance; store, covered, at room temperature.

2. To make the crust, whisk the flour, sugar, lemon zest, and salt in a large bowl until uniform. Add the butter; use a pastry cutter, a fork, or two knives to cut the butter into the flour, continually working the butter through the mixture until it all resembles coarse sand.

3. Stir in the eggs; stir until the dough gathers into a ball. Seal in plastic wrap and refrigerate for at least 30 minutes or up to 24 hours.

4. Position the rack in the center of the oven and preheat the oven to 350°F.

5. Unwrap the dough and cut it into two even pieces. Lightly flour a clean work surface; set the dough on top. Lightly flour the dough and a rolling pin; roll the dough into an 11-inch circle. Set the dough into a 10-inch tart pan with a removable bottom, pressing it against the fluted edges to make an even crust. Spread the blueberry jam over the crust.

6. Set the second piece of dough onto a lightly floured work surface; flour the dough and a rolling pin. Roll the dough into a 10-inch circle. Use a fluted pastry cutter, a pizza wheel, or a knife to cut ½-inch-thick strips; lay these over the tart, forming a crosshatch design. Seal the edges of the crust.

7. Bake until the crust is golden brown, about 40 minutes. Transfer to a wire rack and let cool to room temperature, about 2 hours. Remove the sides from the tart pan and slice into wedges to serve. Garnish with whipped cream, if desired.

CHOCOLATE RICE CROSTATA

CROSTATA DI RISO E CIOCCOLATO

8 servings

ADELINA ORAZZO ✳ In Milan, I discovered fruit *crostatas*. When I returned to Naples, I taught everyone I knew how to make them, including this less common variation.

FOR THE FILLING
2 cups whole **milk**
1 cup superfino **arborio rice**
¼ cup **sugar**
¼ cup **glacéed orange peel**, chopped
3 ounces bittersweet **chocolate**, melted and cooled

1 large **egg** plus 1 large **egg yolk**, at room, temperature, lightly beaten
2 tablespoons unsalted **butter**, melted and cooled
¼ teaspoon **salt**

FOR THE CRUST
1⅔ cups **all-purpose flour**, plus more for rolling
10 tablespoons (1¼ sticks) unsalted **butter**, softened, plus more for greasing

6 tablespoons **sugar**
2 large **egg yolks**
2 teaspoons finely grated **lemon zest**
1 teaspoon **vanilla extract**
¼ teaspoon **salt**

1. To make the filling, mix the milk and rice in a large saucepan and bring to a boil, stirring occasionally. Cover, reduce the heat, and simmer until the liquid is absorbed and the rice is tender, about 20 minutes. Transfer to a large bowl and let cool for 30 minutes.

2. To make the crust, put the flour, butter, sugar, egg yolks, lemon zest, vanilla, and salt in a large bowl and beat with a handheld mixer at medium speed until well blended. Gather into a ball, seal in plastic wrap, and refrigerate for 30 minutes or up to 24 hours.

3. Set the dough on a lightly floured surface. Roll the dough into a 12-inch circle. Press into the pie plate. Trim off the excess and reserve. Pinch and flute the edge.

4. Position the rack in the center of the oven and preheat the oven to 350°F. Lightly butter a 9-inch pie plate.

5. To continue making the filling, stir the sugar, orange peel, chocolate, eggs, butter, and salt into the rice until uniform. Spread the rice filling onto the crust.

6. Roll the reserved dough to ¼ inch thick and cut out small circles. Lay the circles over the filling. Bake until lightly golden, about 30 minutes. Let cool on a wire rack, about 2 hours. Slice into wedges to serve.

XI

PIATTI TIPICI delle FESTE

JODY SCARAVELLA *In Italy, there seems to be a holiday, celebrated with traditional foods, almost every month. Perhaps the most beloved one with a distinctive menu is Christmas Eve, celebrated with an array of fish dishes in many, but not all, regions. Most of the dishes customarily served on Christmas Eve and other holidays are as likely to show up on the dinner table any night of the week. This chapter features dishes made only for specific holidays.*

Margherita Amato

I come from Casteldaccia, a coastal town in the province of Palermo, Sicily. When I was growing up, there were probably about eight thousand inhabitants; now it's almost a small city. The heart of the town

With my brother and my favorite doll, 1952

is the modest castle of the family who launched the Sicilian wine industry in the early nineteenth century, the dukes of Salaparuta, and remains known for Vino Corvo, among other famous lines.

My great-grandfather, along with his five sons, built a business crafting barrels for the wineries. The huge barrel workshop was a block from where I grew up. We were closely entwined with our neighbors, most of whom were coworkers or blood relatives. Those bonds were reinforced because they shopped at the grocery store that my mother ran on the ground floor of our house.

That's where I first learned about werewolves. Our neighbor Grazia's husband was afflicted, and when he had a spell, she'd come by to describe it to my mother. "Lock the door," he'd tell Grazia. "Don't open it, no matter what, even if you hear scratching or banging. I could hurt you . . ." My mother hung on every word, and so did I, at five or six years old, keeping her company in the store. Grazia's husband would flee to the countryside until he recovered his human form. Only then, when he called to her in a normal voice, could she unlock the door.

This was not the only werewolf incident. Parents warned their kids that, when the moon was full, if they saw someone strange, they should immediately run to where the streets crossed. Werewolves were known to fear crossroads. There were so many stories, and everyone gave the same description of the werewolf's howl: a deep, penetrating animal cry that would chill your blood. In Casteldaccia—perhaps in Sicily—werewolves were just one of the many mysteries of our world.

Most of the houses in Casteldaccia were attached, three or four stories high, and made of stucco or yellow brick, made and laid by hand. The streets are cramped and narrow, but lemon and olive trees grow everywhere. Close to the outskirts of town are the separate, gated villas, and beyond them lies the countryside, where my parents owned some land. A lot of vegetables grown on the land were sold in my mother's store, along with fresh eggs, cheese, ricotta, and cold cuts supplied by local farmers.

The youngest of four children and the only girl, I was like the princess of my family. We lived comfortably, thanks to my mother's store and the family barrel factory, so I never had household responsibilities. In fact, I had especially smooth hands, which people would always compliment. If I even offered to help wash dishes, my mom would protest, "Oh no, you'll ruin your soft, beautiful hands."

But from the time I was tiny, I was curious about cooking. My mother would give me little kitchen jobs, and I still remember my first creation, a small fried pizza with tomatoes, onions, and anchovies—the kind we make for holidays, called *sfincione*. We make a special version of these pizzas, with anchovies rolled right into the dough for Carnevale, the period leading up to Lent.

I loved Carnevale. On weekends, people with large homes or even garages would throw them open to everyone—families, friends, and strangers—who would go from house to house to dance. Wherever you wound up at midnight, you'd sit down to eat, like one big family. It was magical.

Then, in the middle of Lent, comes St. Joseph's Day, March 19. In Casteldaccia we credit St. Joseph (our town's and also Sicily's patron saint) with saving us from privation. Casteldaccia borders on the sea and then stretches into the mountains, where we grow food crops. When a long drought was parching the mountainside, the desperate farmers prayed to St. Joseph. Finally, the rains came. In gratitude, the people pledged, from then on, to celebrate St. Joseph by making pasta with sardines, combining the fruits of the sea and of the land (especially the wild fennel that is our special, local addition). The whole town cooked and ate together. Other Sicilians have their own St. Joseph's Day legends, but everyone seems to serve sardines, as well as *sfinge di San Giuseppe*, a fried pastry with sweet ricotta filling.

All these holidays hold joy for me. I remember being eight or nine years old and joining all the women in the kitchen—my mother, my aunts, my cousins, all much older than me—and feeling like I was being initiated into age-old cooking rituals.

One of our traditional dishes was called *baccalà apparecchiato*. *Baccalà*, of course, is dried, salted cod that comes in a slab, which you reconstitute by soaking it for a day or more in several changes of water. *Apparecchiato* means "set," as in "setting the table," or already soaked and ready to serve, once it was cooked. We'd flour and fry the baccalà, then lay it on tray, covered with a sauce of tomatoes, capers, olives, pre-boiled chopped celery, and a shot of vinegar to give it zing.

Another regional classic was *panelle*, chickpea flour cooked with fennel seeds and water to form a paste, then turned out to cool in a thin layer on a marble slab. When the paste solidified, it was cut into squares and fried until crispy. Panelle are delicious—and addictive. In some towns, they're traditionally served on December 8, the *Festa della Madonna*, or the Feast of the Immaculate Conception. It's the holiday that kicks off the Christmas season, running through January 6, the Feast of the Epiphany.

It's a whole month of celebration. The second milestone of the month, December 13, is the Feast of St. Lucy. A martyr of the early Christian church, she is the patron saint of Syracuse, Sicily. According to legend, the city was suffering a terrible famine. People were starving until, on December 13, a ship pulled into the harbor, loaded with grain. Being so hungry, they couldn't take time to mill and leaven the grain for bread. So instead they dragged huge pots into the streets and, over open fires, boiled the grain until it was soft enough to eat. So many lives were saved that, on every December 13, the population vowed to eat boiled grains and other plain foods, avoiding anything leavened with yeast, to honor and thank St. Lucy.

Other traditional foods for St. Lucy's Day include boiled potatoes, plain chickpeas, and rice balls (which are fancier but still count as grain). We take the feast day very seriously. Here's a funny story: Late one December 12, when my mother and I were preparing our grain dishes together, my young daughter, who'd been helping, felt hungry. She asked for a salami sandwich. "Of course," I said, "but you'd better hurry. You can't eat bread after midnight." I lopped off a piece of focaccia, slicing it open, but then caught sight of the clock. "Quick!" I said, and she jammed it into her mouth. She finished chewing just in time. Then we both burst out laughing—I was so anxious for her to gulp the bread before midnight that we forgot the salami.

St. Lucy's Day begins the countdown to Christmas. Around then, we start making *buccellati*, the traditional fig-filled

Coopers in Casteldaccia, 1945

TARALLI

ADELINA ORAZZO

One of our holiday essentials was *taralli*, a ring-shaped snack that was like a cross between a bagel and an unsalted pretzel. When I was young, women would come down from the mountainside with huge baskets of taralli balanced on their heads. Most of them didn't own shoes, so in town they'd wear layers of socks, tied with string around their ankles, to keep them on their feet. They'd go from door to door selling the taralli, and everyone would buy enough to last for a week of entertaining.

When holiday visitors arrived, we'd always set out some salami and cheese, along with plate of taralli and a bowl of water. The water was necessary because the taralli were so hard that they needed a quick dip to soften them.

Sicilian pastry that has counterparts all over Italy. When I was growing up, we'd have a buccellati competition, to see whose batch was most attractive and best tasting. I love doing that today with my daughters and grandkids—it's like a big family party. We go through something like three pounds of flour, baking buccellati to serve to holiday guests and give to friends.

For Christmas Eve, our traditional food was sfincione, maybe along with some seafood that we didn't get every day, like mussels, clams, and octopus. But having fish for Christmas Eve, as many Italians do, wasn't a priority for people in my town or my family, as much as having our sfincione.

There were also a lot of fried vegetables on our Christmas Eve table, delicious ones that are a lot of work to make. Cardoons, for example, have spiky strands that have to be stripped out, like removing the strings from a celery stalk. Our other favorite Christmas dish was Sicilian lasagna, a baked pasta made with *anelletti* or "little rings." We'd line the dish with tomato sauce cooked with chopped veal and pork, plus peas; add a layer of parboiled anelletti, top that with mozzarella, ham or prosciutto, and quartered hard-boiled eggs; then keep layering. The dish is a showstopper, a real extravaganza.

And on New Year's Eve, everything we eat is lucky. We start with a green vegetable, typically broccoli rabe, and then have lentils—very important!—followed by all kinds of fish. According to folk wisdom, these foods bring prosperity in the year ahead because they have the color or shape of money.

For much of my life, I've been what you could call binational, dividing my time between Sicily and the United States. Two of my older brothers immigrated to America, and when I was twenty, my parents planned to join them. But one day, when I was hanging out in my mother's store, a guy stopped in to buy a bag of chips. He was from Termini Imerese, a town about twenty minutes down the coast. Apparently he'd noticed me before because he left a note, saying, "I like you very much and want to meet you."

How romantic! But it was February, and in May we were moving to New York. The last thing my mother wanted was for me to fall in love. But Giuseppe (nicknamed Pino) didn't give up, saying, "I can't stand to lose you." One Sunday, Pino was waiting outside our church after mass. He took my hand and said, "Let's get in the car." When I did, he announced, "We're leaving," and took off. Just like that, we got married.

My elopement shocked the family. But finally the dust settled, especially after the birth of my first child, Vincenza, who we call Cinzia, a couple of years later. I was in

LA VIGILIA

ROSARIA VIGORITO   We wait all year for our Christmas Eve dinner, which is such a feast that it's almost ridiculous with the food. My mother makes the traditional Feast of the Seven Fishes or *La Vigilia*, the vigil kept while waiting for Jesus to be born. Or, at least, having seven fishes is our tradition. In some families, you just have to eat an odd number, and in others the number doesn't matter, as long as you eat fish.

ELVIRA PANTALEO   Many Italians eat only fish on Christmas Eve, but our tradition was the opposite. We'd eat our fish on Christmas Day. For New Year's Eve, we'd also roast a big fish, often *cernia*, or a big grouper, to eat with mussels and clams. On the side we had traditional foods for luck, like figs, nuts, and lentils but never the cotechino they eat in northern Italy. Who needs sausage when you have the best fish imaginable?

America on vacation when, four years later, my second daughter, Liliana, was born. Over the next decade, we lived mostly in Sicily but spent enough time in New York that my daughters got Americanized. I think it enriched their lives to experience the way I grew up, or what remained of it.

During Carnevale, 1960

One example: they got to see people bring fresh olives to the press on the hillside above our house. When I was young, it took hard labor to run the press—two giant wheel-like stones, pushed by strong men—but by the 1980s, it was motorized. The oil would stream into a collection basin, then was scooped into double-handled jars or tins, wide at the bottom to trap sediment. My daughter Liliana, especially, remembers the strong, earthy smell of the press, and how good the oil tasted, with a few anchovies on *schiacciata*, our local flatbread.

But there are advantages to living in America, especially for young people. If you speak English, the jobs are better, and there's just more going on. It's hectic, while in Sicily, life has a quiet rhythm. You wake up, clean the house, cook for lunch, take an afternoon nap, and then start planning dinner. You think, "Maybe I'll drop in on my cousin on the way to the butcher." The same thing day after day—it's comforting and enjoyable, but it can get boring after a while, even for me nowadays.

I wasn't surprised when my daughters married and decided to move to America; I followed when the grandkids came along. They call me Nonnina, which means "little grandmother," to distinguish me from my mother, Nonna Lilla. One of my grandsons, Alex, is interested in cooking; and on holidays my granddaughter Christina loves to join me, her mother, and her aunt in the kitchen to learn the traditional dishes. My other grandsons, Giuseppe and Nicholas, do their part by enjoying what we make.

I love going to Sicily for a few months a year, to see the extended family. But I really have a whole life here now, which I enjoy. The grandkids mean the world to me, of course, but I've even gotten used to New York. It gets your blood boiling. It keeps you young.

EASTER BREAD LA TAGLIATA DI PASQUA

 ──────────────────────────────── *8 servings* ├──┤

ADELINA ORAZZO ✳ Italian Easter breads vary from region to region, town to town, and even family to family. Some are savory, like this one; others are sweet. On Easter morning, we serve this bread on a festive platter with slices of soppressata, *ricotta salata*, fennel, and hard-boiled eggs.

⅔ cup warm **milk** (105° to 115°F)
¼ cup **sugar**
1 (¼ ounce) package active dry **yeast** (2¼ teaspoons)
8 tablespoons (1 stick) unsalted **butter**, melted and cooled to room temperature, plus more for greasing
3 large **eggs**, at room temperature
½ teaspoon **salt**
2⅓ cups **all-purpose flour**, plus more for dusting and kneading

4 ounces **salumi, soppressata** or **prosciutto cotto**, or a mixture, casings removed and meat diced
1 ounce finely grated **Pecorino Romano** (about ¼ cup)
1 ounce finely grated **Grana Padano** (about ¼ cup)
3 large hard-boiled **eggs**
Sliced **soppressata**, for garnish
Shaved **ricotta salata**, for garnish
Trimmed, sliced **fennel** bulb, for garnish

1. Whisk the milk, sugar, and yeast in a small bowl and set aside until foamy, about 5 minutes. Whisk in the butter, 2 eggs, and salt until uniform. Stir in the flour until a soft dough forms. Lightly dust a work surface with flour, turn the dough out onto it, and knead for 10 minutes, until smooth and elastic. Gather the dough into a ball.

2. Lightly butter a large bowl, set the dough in it, and turn over to coat in the butter. Cover with a clean kitchen towel and set aside in a warm, draft-free place until doubled in bulk, about 1½ hours.

3. Turn the dough out onto a lightly floured work surface. Flatten the dough; add the salumi, Pecorino Romano, and Grano Padano, and knead lightly until well incorporated. Divide the dough into two equal pieces; roll each piece into a 14-inch-long strand. Pinch these two strands together at one end, then twist them together six times lengthwise to make a single coiled strand. Form the strand into a circle and pinch the ends to seal.

4. Lightly butter a large rimmed baking sheet. Transfer the coiled ring to it. Press the hard-boiled eggs at three equidistant spots around the coil, using the natural indentations caused by the crossing of the strands.

5. Whisk the remaining egg and 2 tablespoons water in a small bowl until foamy. Brush lightly over the bread. Cover with a clean kitchen towel and set aside in a warm, draft-free place until doubled in size, about 1 hour. Meanwhile, position the rack in the center of the oven and preheat the oven to 350°F.

6. Bake until golden brown and hollow-sounding when tapped, 25 to 30 minutes. Transfer to a wire rack to cool for 15 minutes or to room temperature, about 1 hour. To serve, slice the bread into wedges and surround these on a platter with soppressata, ricotta salata, and sliced fennel for garnish.

WHEAT BERRY PUDDING FOR ST. LUCY'S DAY

CUCCIA DI SANTA LUCIA

 6 servings

MARGHERITA AMATO ✳ On December 13, we honor St. Lucy, who, according to legend, saved people from starvation by sending a ship full of grain. *Cuccia* can be a main course, with the addition of fava beans or chickpeas, but my family prefers this sweeter version topped with chocolate shavings.

1¼ cups soft white spring **wheat berries**
1 medium **orange**
1 (2-inch) **cinnamon** stick
1 teaspoon **salt**
1 cup whole **milk**

3 tablespoons **sugar**
1 teaspoon ground **cinnamon**
Finely chopped **candied butternut squash**, for garnish
Dark **chocolate** shavings, for garnish

1. Soak the wheat berries in a large bowl of water at room temperature for 24 hours. Meanwhile, remove wide strips of the orange peel (but not the white pith) with a vegetable peeler.

2. Drain the wheat berries in a fine-mesh sieve or a large colander lined with paper towels. Place in a large saucepan and cover with water by 3 inches. Stir in the orange peel, cinnamon stick, and salt; bring to a boil. Reduce the heat to medium, set a lid askew on the pan, and cook until very tender, about 1 hour.

3. Drain again; discard the orange peel and cinnamon stick. Wipe out the saucepan and return the wheat berries to it. Stir in the milk and bring to a boil over medium-high heat. Cook, stirring often, until thick and rich, about 10 minutes.

4. Scrape and pour the wheat berries into six ramekins; let cool for 10 minutes. Mix the sugar and ground cinnamon in a small bowl and sprinkle on top. Garnish with candied butternut squash and chocolate.

EASTER WHEAT PIE PASTIERA NAPOLETANA DI GRANO

 8 servings

CARMELINA PICA ✳ To make this traditional Easter pie, you can buy presoaked wheat at Italian specialty stores. If you prefer, you can soak the dry wheat yourself by covering it with cold water and boiling for 15 minutes until the husks crack open. Then remove from the heat and continue soaking for 24 hours. Remove the husks before using.

FOR THE WHEAT BERRIES
1 cup soft white spring **wheat berries**
1 teaspoon **salt**
½ cup whole **milk**
1 teaspoon **granulated sugar**

¼ cup finely chopped **glacéed orange peel**
¼ cup finely chopped **glacéed citron**

FOR THE PASTRY
2 cups **all-purpose flour**, plus more for rolling
½ cup **granulated sugar**
½ teaspoon **salt**
8 tablespoons (1 stick) unsalted **butter**,

diced and chilled, plus more for greasing
3 large **eggs**, at room temperature
1 tablespoon whole **milk**, if needed

FOR THE FILLING
4 cups whole-milk **ricotta**
1½ cups **granulated sugar**
4 large **eggs**, at room temperature, separated, plus 2 large **egg yolks**

1 tablespoon finely grated **orange zest**
⅓ cup fresh **orange juice**
1 teaspoon **vanilla extract**
1 teaspoon **rum**

Confectioners' sugar, for garnish

1. To make the wheat berries, place the wheat berries in a large bowl, cover with cool water, and soak for 24 hours.

2. Drain the wheat berries in a fine-mesh sieve or a large colander lined with paper towels. Transfer to a large saucepan; cover with water until they're submerged by 3 inches. Stir in the salt and bring to a boil. Reduce the heat to medium, set a cover askew over the pan, and simmer until very tender, about 1 hour. Drain in a sieve, wipe out the saucepan, and return the wheat berries to it.

3. Stir in the milk and granulated sugar. Bring to a boil over medium-high heat, stirring occasionally. Cook until thick and rich, about 5 minutes, stirring occasionally. Remove

the pan from the heat; stir in the orange peel and citron. Let cool to room temperature, about 1 hour.

4. To make the pastry, sift the flour, granluated sugar, and salt into a large bowl. Add the chilled butter and use a pastry cutter or a fork to cut it into the flour mixture until the combined mixture resembles coarse sand.

5. Stir in the eggs, one at a time. Continue stirring until the mixture forms a soft dough. If it's too dry, add the milk to help it come together. Turn the dough out on a lightly floured work surface. Knead until smooth, about 2 minutes. Seal in plastic wrap and refrigerate for 30 minutes.

6. Position the rack in the middle of the oven and preheat the oven to 350°F. Lightly butter a 10-inch pie plate.

7. Unwrap the dough and divide it into three equal pieces. Lightly flour a work surface, press two of the pieces back together, and roll into a 12-inch circle. Transfer to the pie plate with a ½-inch overhang. Cover with a clean kitchen towel.

8. To make the filling, beat the ricotta and granulated sugar in a large bowl with a hand-held mixer on medium speed until creamy, about 3 minutes. Beat in 6 egg yolks until smooth, then beat in the orange zest, orange juice, vanilla, and rum. Stir in the reserved wheat berry mixture.

9. Clean and dry the beaters. Beat the 4 egg whites in a large clean bowl with the mixer on high speed until soft peaks form. Fold the beaten whites into the wheat berry mixture, using a rubber spatula with wide, gentle arcs to keep their loft. Pour into the piecrust; smooth the top.

10. Roll out the remaining dough on a lightly floured surface into a 10-inch circle. Cut into ¾-inch-wide strips and arrange these as a crosshatch on the pie. Fold the crust overhang onto the top of the pie, thereby hiding (and sealing) the ends of the lattice strips.

11. Bake until firm and golden brown, about 1 hour. Transfer to a wire rack and let cool to room temperature, about 1 hour. Slice into wedges and sprinkle with confectioners' sugar.

CHICKPEA FRITTERS PANELLE

8 servings

MARGHERITA AMATO ✳ These addictive fritters are traditionally eaten on December 8, the Feast of the Immaculate Conception, which kicks off the Christmas season.

4 cups **chickpea flour**
1 teaspoon **salt**, plus more for serving
½ teaspoon **fennel seeds**
½ teaspoon freshly ground **black pepper**

Canola or **vegetable oil**, for greasing and frying
Fresh **lemon juice**, for serving

1. Lightly grease a 9 x 13-inch baking dish, preferably one with squared corners for fritters with an even shape.

2. Bring 6 cups water to a boil in a large saucepan. Stir in the chickpea flour, salt, fennel seeds, and pepper. Pour, spread, and press the mixture into the baking dish, smoothing the top with a rubber spatula. Let cool to room temperature, about 2 hours.

3. Turn the chickpea rectangle out onto a large cutting board; remove the baking dish. Slice into eight even rectangles, 4½ x 3¼ inches each.

4. Spread paper towels on your work surface and set a wire rack on top. Pour the oil into a large skillet to a depth of ¼ inch and set over medium heat until rippling. Add four chickpea rectangles; fry until golden brown, turning once, about 4 minutes. Transfer to the wire rack. Add more oil to bring the depth back to ¼ inch, then fry the remaining chickpea rectangles as before. Sprinkle with salt and lemon juice immediately and serve hot.

ACKNOWLEDGMENTS

Heartfelt gratitude goes to Leslie Meredith, our nurturing and patient editor at Simon & Schuster, and Judith Curr, our wonderfully supportive publisher. Donna Loffredo has also been an incredible pillar of support.

Others at Simon & Schuster who deserve our deep appreciation include: Lisa Sciambra, publicist; Dana Sloan, interior art director; Suet Chong, interior designer; Stacey Kulig, production manager; Jackie Jou, marketing manager; Lauren Shakeley, consultant; and Jeanne Lee, jacket art director; along with those laboring behind the scenes who have given us the gifts of their talents and hard work.

The members of the team who made this book possible are Frances Janisch, photographer, who created its beautiful images; Marianna Vasquez, who did the food styling; and the crew who stepped in at the eleventh hour to develop, test, and write the recipes.

On a more personal note, I thank agents Jeff Silberman and Frank Weimann, formerly of the Literary Group, now part of Folio Management. This book never would have come to life without their faith and efforts.

I am grateful to Elisa Petrini, my coauthor and now friend, for guiding me with unflagging enthusiasm though the mysterious process of creating a book, along with capturing the spirited voices of the nonnas and the magic of the Enoteca. Her aunt, Alma Petrini, not only contributed invaluable translation help for both nonna interviews and recipes, but became another member of the Enoteca family.

Much love to Michela Traetto, my wife (aka the Nonna Whisperer), whose contribution to this effort cannot be overstated—translating,

organizing, persuading, and boosting morale are just the beginning—and who has granted me the most precious gift, sharing her life with me.

I am indebted to my customers at the Enoteca for their support, sustaining the dream for all these years, and for the joy they've given me during this journey.

Finally, my greatest debt is to the nonnas, who embody a vanishing tradition—not just my own, which once seemed lost with the passing of my family, but of people of every heritage who've been buoyed by a grandmother's love.

INDEX

Fig Cookies, 229–31, *230*
fish:
    appetizers, *see* antipasti
    Branzino in a Salt Crust with
        Lemon and Oregano
        Sauce, 182
    Bream in Potato Crust, *186*, 187
    on Christmas Eve, 193, 253
    Dried, Polenta with
        Cauliflower and, 82
    La Vigilia, 254
    Pappardelle with Salmon,
        Zucchini, and Walnuts,
        124, 125
    Sicilian-Style Salt Cod with
        Raisins, Tomatoes, and
        Olives, *178*, 179
    Soup Palermo Style, 175
    Stuffed Sardines *34*, 35
    Stuffed Swordfish Rolls, *184*,
        185
    see also fish courses
fish and seafood, pasta dishes
        with:
    Calamarata with Mussels and
        Eggplant, 127
    Fresh Fettuccine with Tuna,
        Eggplant, and Mint, 123
    Lagane and Chickpeas with
        Shrimp, 126
    Linguine with Cuttlefish and
        Its Ink, 132, *133*
    Linguine with Octopus Sauce,
        130, 131
    Pappardelle with Salmon,
        Zucchini, and Walnuts,
        124, 125
    Scialatielli with Clams,
        Mussels, and Crab, 128, *129*
    Spaghetti with Sea Urchins, 121
    Ziti with Fresh Sardines,
        Fennel, and Breadcrumbs,
        122

fish courses, 175–87
    Branzino in a Salt Crust with
        Lemon and Oregano
        Sauce, 183
    Bream in Potato Crust, *186*, 187
    Calamari, Stuffed, 177
    Cuttlefish or Baby Squid,
        Sautéed, 176
    Eels in Wine and Garlic
        Sauce, 180, *181*
    Fish Soup Palermo Style, 175
    Salt Cod with Raisins,
        Tomatoes, and Olives,
        Sicilian-Style, *178*, 179
    Swordfish Rolls, Stuffed, 184, *185*
    Tuna Fillets with Onions and
        Vinegar, Sicilian-Style, 182
fontina, in Stuffed Fried Dough
        Crescents, 147
fritters:
    Chickpea, *262*, 263
    Vegetable, with Two Batters,
        70, 71–72
frittole, 9

G
gnocchi, 79, 225
    Potato, in Meat Sauce with
        Rolled Beef, *90*, 91–92
    Potato, with Porcini and
        Broccolini, 93, *94*
    Ricotta, in Tomato Sauce, *94*,
        95–96
Gorgonzola, 78, 79
    Fennel with, 68, *69*
    Penne with Radicchio,
        Walnuts and, *116*, 117
    Sauce, 214

H
ham:
    Neapolitan Potato Pie, 58, *59*
    Sicilian Lasagna, 167

harvest, preserving for winter,
        10, 104
herbs, 104–5, 192
Herring, Smoked, Salad with
        Oranges, 38
holiday specialties:
    Chickpea Fritters, *262*, 263
    Easter Bread, *256*, 257–58
    Easter Wheat Pie, 260–61
    Wheat Berry Pudding for St.
        Lucy's Day, 259
Honey-Glazed Dough Balls, 232
hunting, 9, 80

I
Immaculate Conception, Feast of,
        229, 252
    Chickpea Fritters for, *262*, 263

L
Lagane and Chickpeas with
        Shrimp, 126
lamb, 43, 106, 192
    Head, Baked, 218, *219*
    Rack of, with Tomatoes and
        Potatoes, *216*, 217
    Stew with Creamy Cheese
        Sauce, 215
lard, 8–9, 192
    Roasted Pork Loin with
        Oranges, 208
lasagna, 140, 162, 191, 253
    Meat and Three-Cheese, with
        Eggplant, Asparagus, and
        Peas, My Prizewinning,
        164, 165–66
    noodles, in Lagane and
        Chickpeas with Shrimp, 126
    Pasticcio with Béchamel and
        Bolognese Sauce, 162–63
    Sicilian, 167
Lemon and Oregano Sauce, 183
Lentils, Cotechino and, 207